D:

First
Plac _____ ___ferred to
the _____ ...tre, London in May 1977 where it received
exce....onally high praise from a wide range of critics. The
production established David Edgar as a major playwright, one of
the most important of the young generation of dramatists to
emerge out of the 'portable' theatre movement of the late sixties.

1947. The Twilight of Empire in India. Sergeant Turner and
his Colonel share a bottle of whisky in reluctant celebration of
Independence. 'Do you think Mr Churchill will do anything
about it, sir? When the Conservatives get back in?'

1976. A bye-election in the West Midlands against the background
of an industrial dispute involving Asian labour. A three-cornered
fight between Labour, Conservative (candidate: the Colonel's
nephew) and the up and coming Nation Forward party
(candidate: Sergeant, now Mr Turner) — a contest in which the
issue of race cuts like a razor through the conventional cosy
assumptions of British politics, with alarming and prophetic
results.

It is impossible to read David Edgar's play without feeling
provoked into re-examining one's own political sentiments.
Impossible also not to admire the skill with which he has woven
so many strands into an authentic, gripping and theatrically
effective play of impressive scope and power.

'. . . the supreme virtue of this rackingly eloquent and vitally
important play is that it explores the impulses behind British
Fascism with real insight. . . and shows the mixed and muddled
motives that generate right-wing extremism. . . the final effect
is of a play that is something more than skilful and well-written.
It is one that is actually necessary.'

Michael Billington, *The Guardian*

'I cannot remember any play that coupled so much urgent topical
information with such dramatic force.'

Irving Wardle, *The Times*

'It is . . . the panoramic political play that writers of Mr Edgar's
generation have been straining after for years.'

Robert Cushman, *The Observer*

by the same author

WRECKERS (Eyre Methuen, 1977)

DICK DETERRED (Monthly Review Press, New York, 1974)

TWO KINDS OF ANGEL (The London Fringe Theatre, Burnham House, 1975)

MARY BARNES (Eyre Methuen, 1979)

TEENDREAMS (Eyre Methuen, 1979)

David Edgar

DESTINY

EYRE METHUEN · LONDON

First published in Methuen New Theatrescripts
in 1976 by Eyre Methuen Ltd, 11 New Fetter Lane,
London EC4P 4EE
Reprinted in Methuen Modern Plays 1978
Reprinted 1979
Copyright ©1976 by David Edgar
ISBN 0 413 38910 3

Set IBM by 𝍐 Tek-Art, Croydon, Surrey
Printed in Great Britain by Fakenham Press Ltd, Fakenham, Norfolk

To Ron and Di

Destiny could not have been written without the help and advice of many people, including the staff of the Institute of Race Relations; Maurice Ludmer and Gerry Gable of Searchlight magazine; Benny Bunsee; Don Milligan; and, especially, Sue Clegg.

DE

DESTINY was first presented by the Royal Shakespeare Company at the Other Place, Stratford-upon-Avon, on 22 September 1976. The production transferred to the Aldwych Theatre, London on 12 May 1977, with the following cast:

TURNER	Ian McDiarmid
GURJEET SINGH KHERA	Marc Zuber
COLONEL CHANDLER	David Lyon
MAJOR ROLFE	Michael Pennington
PETER CROSBY	Paul Shelley
PLATT	Clyde Pollitt
MRS CHANDLER	Judith Harte
FRANK KERSHAW	Dennis Clinton
BOB CLIFTON	Paul Moriarty
SANDY CLIFTON	Frances Viner
PAUL	Greg Hicks
TONY	Leonard Preston
MONTY GOODMAN	Paul Shelley
DAVID MAXWELL	John Nettles
RICHARD CLEAVER	Bob Peck
DRUMONT	David Lyon
PRAKASH PATEL	Dev Sagoo
ATTWOOD	David Lyon
MRS HOWARD	Judith Harte
LIZ	Cherie Lunghi
INSPECTOR	Hubert Rees
EMMA CROSBY	Judy Monahan
DIANA WILCOX	Denyse Alexander
CAROL	Cherie Lunghi
PARTYGOERS/MEMBERS	Denyse Alexander
OF THE PATRIOTIC	Michael Cashman
LEAGUE/POLICE	Jack Galloway
	Alfred Molina
	Judy Monahan
	Martin Read
	Hubert Rees

Directed by Ron Daniels
Designed by Di Seymour
Lighting by Leo Leibovici

The constituency of Taddley, where most of the play is set, is a fictional town to the west of Birmingham.

The Nation Forward Party, the Taddley Patriotic League, the Association of Diecasters and Foundrymen, the Baron Castings Co. Ltd, the United Vehicle Corporation and the Metropolitan Investment Trust are fictional organisations.

None of the characters seen in the play has ever existed.

ACT ONE

'The Conservative Party by long tradition and settled belief is the Party of the Empire. We are proud of its past. We see it as the surest hope in our day. We proclaim our abiding faith in its destiny.'

Conservative Party Manifesto
General Election, 1950

'The Right is acutely aware that the kind of Britain it wishes to preserve very largely depends on Britain remaining a great power. . . Everything about the British class system begins to look foolish and tacky when related to a second-class power on the decline.'

Peregrine Worsthorne,
Conservative commentator,
April 1959

Act One

Scene One

Darkness. We hear a sonorous VOICE:

VOICE. Long years ago, we made a tryst with destiny, and now the time comes when we shall redeem our pledge, not wholly or in full measure, but very substantially. A moment comes, which comes but rarely in history, when we step out from the old to the new, when an age ends, and when the soul of a nation, long oppressed, finds utterance. At the stroke of the midnight hour, when the world sleeps, India will awake to life and freedom.

Slight pause.

Jawaharlal Pandit Nehru, 14th August, 1947.

Lights snap up, and with them, sounds of celebration in the distance. We are in the box room of a British Army barracks, near Jullundur in the Punjab. On the back wall hangs a huge, dark painting of the putting down of the Indian Mutiny. It dominates the set. A door to one side, two chairs, several packing cases, a stuffed tiger, a trunk, all covered with dust sheets. A British Army Sergeant, in tropical uniform, stands by the door. He has just switched the light on. His name is TURNER; *he is from the West Midlands, about 20, and harrassed.*

TURNER. Oh, bloody hell. (*Exit. Shouts, off.*) Khera! Khera! (*Pause.*) For Christ's sake, Khera, where the bloody hell you hiding?

Sound of running feet. The voice of a young Indian:

KHERA. Sir?

TURNER. Where the hell you been? (*Pause.*) Aw, come on. Look what I found.

TURNER *comes back into the room with* GURJEET SINGH KHERA, *an 18-year-old Sikh servant, who wears a turban, and has a steel bangle on his wrist and a knife at his belt. When talking to* KHERA, TURNER *speaks loudly and slowly.*

TURNER. Right. See this stuff? It's going. Out. You, me, get this stuff out, right? (KHERA *nods and does nothing.*) Well, come on, let's get weaving. Get these sheets off, see what we got. (KHERA *and* TURNER *begin pulling sheets off furniture and packing cases.* KHERA *is just dropping the sheets.* TURNER *notices.*) Hey, you. Don't just drop 'em anywhere. Fold 'em up. (KHERA *does nothing.* TURNER *waves his folded sheet as an example.*) Fold, yuh? Savvy? (KHERA *nods wisely.*) Well, get a move on, then. (KHERA, *still nodding, starts folding a sheet, very slowly and precisely.*) Jesus Christ.

TURNER *returns to his work. Sounds of celebration, a little louder.*

Your people having a good time then, eh?

Pause.

I said, your people having a good time?

KHERA (*stopping work*). Oh, yes. Having a wizard time. (*As if explaining to a child:*) Independence.

TURNER. Oh, I wondered what it was.

Pause.

All right, get on. (TURNER *pulls the dustsheet off the tiger.*) Now what's this here?

KHERA (*helpfully*). Tiger. Stuffed.

TURNER. You know, I just about worked that out for myself.

KHERA. They shoot them, then they stuff them.

TURNER *looks to heaven, then back to folding. Enter a* COLONEL, *43 years old, upper class.* TURNER *snaps to attention, salutes.*

TURNER. Sir!

COLONEL. It's all right, Sergeant.

TURNER *looks to* KHERA, *who has not responded.* KHERA *becomes aware of his negligence, slowly and lackadaisically comes to attention. Pause. Then:*

Oh, Lord, is this some more?

TURNER. Yes, sir.

COLONEL (*to the tiger*). Ah. What have we here?

KHERA. It's tiger, sir.

TURNER *looking daggers.*

Stuffed.

COLONEL (*smiling*). Yes.

TURNER (*to cover*). I found this trunk, sir, I don't know what. . . .

COLONEL. Do we know whose it is?

TURNER. No, sir. Reckon it's been here a long time. Don't think anyone's been in here for years.

COLONEL. Well, let's take a shufti. Is it open?

TURNER. I'll try it, sir. (TURNER *opens the trunk*. COLONEL *kneels and looks inside*.)

TURNER (*to* KHERA). You can be getting this stuff down to the lorries.

KHERA *is taking the stuff out as:*

COLONEL. Well, well. (*He takes out a red hunting coat*.) Can't jettison the fancy dress, can we?

TURNER. I'm sorry about him, sir, he's —

COLONEL. No matter, Sergeant. After all, it's their day. No doubt all his chums are whooping it up in Jullundur.

TURNER. Yes, sir.

COLONEL. Now, what else . . . ah. (*He takes out a bayonet, desheathes it*.) I'll bet this hasn't seen service for a year or two. (*He looks at the sheath*.) It's certainly not us . . . Indian Army, I'd say . . . (*He shrugs and sheathes the bayonet, puts it back in the trunk. Finds a bottle of whisky*.) Good Lord, it's scotch. That's a turn up for the books. I wonder how long that's been there?

TURNER. Don't know, sir.

COLONEL. Well, it doesn't go off, does it? Where's the boy?

TURNER (*to the door, shouts*). Khera!

KHERA (*off, from a distance*). Sir?

TURNER. Let's have you! Sharpish!

Enter KHERA, *who deliberately speaks to the* COLONEL *rather than to* TURNER.

KHERA. So sorry, sir, I am taking —

COLONEL. Look, will you nip down to the mess and fetch three whisky tumblers. Got that? Say I sent you.

KHERA. Right away, sir. Three tumblers, right sharpish. (*Exit.*)

TURNER. Three, sir?

COLONEL (*stands*). Yes. Why not? (*He shuts the trunk.*) I'm afraid I think we'd better take it all.

TURNER. Yes, sir.

COLONEL. God alone knows where we'll put it.

Slight pause.

TURNER. There been any trouble today, sir?

COLONEL. Not as far as I know. All having a good time. The real shindig here'll be when they decide the boundary. Hence the rush.

TURNER. If you ask me, sir . . . (*He thinks better of it.*)

COLONEL. No, go on.

TURNER. They didn't have all this trouble in the old days, sir. I was in Calcutta last year, the riots, and I can't see they're much more than savages, sir, whatever they say.

COLONEL. Well, ours is not to reason why.

Pause. Enter KHERA *with three tumblers on a tray. He puts them on the trunk.*

Ah, splendid. Do you fancy a tipple, um —

TURNER. Khera, sir.

COLONEL. Khera? (KHERA *doesn't understand.* COLONEL, *waving the bottle:*) Drink?

KHERA. Oh, please, yes.

COLONEL. Splendid. (*He pours the whisky, handing glasses to* KHERA *and* TURNER.) Know what you're going to do when we've all gone home, Khera?

KHERA. Oh, I don't know, sir.

COLONEL. Perhaps you'll come to England one day. See the natives on their own ground, mm?

KHERA. Yes, sir, I would like to come to England very much.

COLONEL. Well, here's to . . . yes, why not. To the King. With whom we need not, I think, couple the name of Mr Attlee.

TURNER. Winston, sir?

COLONEL. Yes, splendid. The King, and Mr Churchill.

They are raising their glasses as MAJOR ROLFE *bursts into the room. He is nearly 30, brusque, and at the moment, in a filthy temper.*

ROLFE. Oh, there you are, Sergeant, I've been looking all over — (*He sees the* COLONEL.) Oh, I'm sorry, Colonel.

COLONEL. That's all right, Major. The Sergeant and I just found ourselves caught up in the general atmosphere of jubilation. Do join us.

COLONEL *nods to* KHERA, *who gives his whisky to* ROLFE. *As* ROLFE *takes it:*

ROLFE. Some bloody wog's whipped the battery from the Landrover.

COLONEL. Oh, not again.

ROLFE. Broad daylight. Anything that isn't nailed down. They've stripped the cellar.

COLONEL. We'll have to do something about the battery.

ROLFE. If we want to get out of here, yes. Your health, Colonel. (*He takes a swig. Slight pause.*)

COLONEL. Your health. (*He and* TURNER *drink.*)

ROLFE (*to* KHERA). Well, don't just stand there gawping. I assume all this stuff's got to be moved?

TURNER. Yes, sir.

ROLFE (*to* KHERA). Well, get moving it.

KHERA (*with a mock salute*). Yes, sir! (*He picks up a packing-case and goes.*)

COLONEL (*refilling glasses*). Quite a bright little chap, that one. Half devil, quite possibly, but hardly half child.

ROLFE. I'm sorry, Colonel?

COLONEL. Kipling. Don't you know it?
   'Take up the White Man's burden —
   Send forth the best ye breed —
   Go, bind your sons to exile
   To serve your captives' need;
   To wait in heavy harness
   On fluttered folk and wild —
   Your new-caught, sullen peoples,
   Half-devil and half-child.'
We used to have to learn it by heart at preparatory school.

ROLFE. I didn't go to a preparatory school, Colonel.

COLONEL. I know you didn't, Major.

ROLFE. Nonetheless, it sounds an eminently appropriate description.

Pause.

TURNER. Is it true, sir, they'll all be able to come to England now, to live?

COLONEL. I believe Mr Attlee is preparing legislation, now India is in the Commonwealth.

ROLFE. Do you approve of that, Colonel?

COLONEL (*quite sharply*). Of course. It's an obligation. We are the mother country, after all.

ROLFE. I have some reservations.

COLONEL. And you're welcome to them.

Pause. The COLONEL *drains his drink.*

I suppose I'd better go and sort out this battery business. See all this stuff gets loaded, Sergeant.

TURNER. Sir.

COLONEL (*meets* KHERA *coming in*). Carry on the good work, Khera.

KHERA *smiles. Exit* COLONEL.

ROLFE. Well, Mr Khera, apparently you've just become a British citizen. (*He pours himself another drink.*)

KHERA. Sir?

ROLFE. Get on with it.

KHERA. Do you want tiger, sir?

ROLFE. Of course we want the bloody tiger. We shot it.

KHERA *takes the tiger out.* ROLFE *takes out his cigarette case, offers it to* TURNER.

Smoke, Sergeant?

TURNER (*not sure of the protocol*). Er . . .

ROLFE. Oh, for Christ's sake, if Mountbatten can hand over the Raj to a bunch of half-crazed dervishes, you can smoke on duty.

TURNER (*takes a cigarette*). Thank you, sir. (*He lights his and*

ROLFE's *cigarette.*) Do you think Mr Churchill will do anything about it, sir? When the Conservatives get back in?

ROLFE. When were you last in England, Sergeant?

TURNER. 1945, sir. Just after VE Day.

ROLFE. A lot has changed.

Slight pause.

TURNER. You going straight back, sir?

ROLFE. No, not straight away. I want to go south, to Tiruppur. Old garrison. Just once, again, before I go.

Enter KHERA.

Well, best get on.

TURNER. Right, sir. Khera, I want the rest of this stuff down in ten minutes.

Pause.

ROLFE. You say 'yes, sir', don't you?

KHERA. Yes, sir.

ROLFE. Let's get this bloody show on the road. (*Exit ROLFE and* TURNER.)

KHERA *goes to the trunk, is about to take the tray off it. Then a second thought, he pours himself a whisky. Then he notices the painting of the Indian Mutiny. He looks at it. He touches the canvas. Then he turns out front, raises the tumbler in a mock toast.*

KHERA. Civis — Brittanicus — Sum.

Blackout and music: Handel's Music for the Royal Fireworks — covers the change.

Scene Two

Dim light on a portrait of the COLONEL, *in uniform, in India. Music fades.*
A spot fades up on the COLONEL, *at the side of the stage. He is very old.*

COLONEL. In '48. Came on home.
　　　　　Colonel Chandler. Monochrome.
　　　　　Another England,
　　　　　Rough and raw,
　　　　　Not gentle, sentimental as before.

Became a politician, not to master but to serve:
To keep a careful finger on the grassroots Tory nerve;
Like any born to riches, not to plunder but to give:
Always a little liberal, a great Conservative.
But as his seat grows marginal, his power's less secure,
His responsive elder statements sound increasingly
     unsure;
Colonel Chandler, past his prime:
Dignified. Worthy. Out of time.
Colonel Chandler, oyster-eyed,
One fine summer morning, died.

*Exit. Lights up, the portrait, we now see, is on the back wall
of a drawing room. A door. A table, with coffee set out, and a
telephone. Enter PETER CROSBY, who is in his late 20s. Like
all the men in this scene, he wears a sober suit and a black tie.
He goes to the telephone, picks it up, dials.*

CROSBY. Extension 237, please. Hallo, Maggie? Look, I'm
at — (*Checks on the phone.*) Taddley 3721. T-A-D-D-L-E-Y.
Well, it's somewhere near West Bromwich. Anyway, I'll be
here 20 minutes, gone an hour, back till about 5.30.
(*Smiles.*) No, it really is a funeral. My uncle.

*Enter PLATT, middle-aged, West Midlands accent, unsure of
his surroundings. About to speak to CROSBY when he sees
he's phoning, so looks at the portrait.*

Hardly. He was very old. Now, look, Maggie, can you get me
running yields on all the Inter-Americans first thing. That's
right. And get Bill to check me futures on the Chicago softs,
sometime before lunch. No, that's all. (*Smiles.*) And you,
sweetheart. (*He puts the phone down, notices PLATT.*)

PLATT. Business goes on, eh, Peter?

CROSBY. I'm afraid the market is no respecter of grief. Coffee?

PLATT. Thanks very much. (CROSBY *pours the coffee.*) We
were all right sorry to see him go.

CROSBY. Yuh. I'd think, actually, you constituency people
knew him rather better than I did.

PLATT. Could be.

CROSBY. Milk and sugar?

PLATT. Just — milk.

CROSBY (*giving PLATT his coffee*). I imagine it was a much
safer seat, in the old days.

PLATT. Oh, ar. Rural, indeed. Now, of course, with the new estates, it's very dodgy.

CROSBY. Did he ever think of retiring?

PLATT. Talking for ten years. But they don't, do they?

CROSBY. Old Tories never die, they just get redistributed.

PLATT *smiles.* CROSBY *looks at his watch.*

Off, soon.

PLATT. Um, Peter, it's probably not the right time to bring it up, but the by-election writ's on the cards any day, and I gather Smith Square were thinking of, keeping it family . . . Perhaps we could have a chat.

CROSBY. Yes, indeed. Why don't we, I'm in no hurry to get back up, have a drink or something afterwards?

PLATT. Fine. We'll go up to the Club. Get your face known.

Slight pause.

Be others in the running, of course. Can't take nepotism to excess.

CROSBY. No, of course. Anything I should push, or steer clear of?

PLATT. Well, I'd keep quiet about Chicago softs, for a start. Concentrate on hards from Longbridge. (CROSBY *smiles.*) Otherwise, bear in mind we're in Enoch country and you'll be all right.

CROSBY. Enoch country?

PLATT. The ground fairly thick with our commonwealth cousins.

CROSBY. Well, yes, on that one, I should make it clear —

PLATT. I shouldn't.

CROSBY. Shouldn't what?

PLATT. Make it clear, cos all they'll say is, you don't have to live with 'em.

CROSBY. Well, yes, but —

KERSHAW *opens the door, lets* MRS CHANDLER *enter and follows her in. They are both in their mid-fifties.*

MRS CHANDLER. Hallo, Peter.

CROSBY (*kisses her*). Aunty.

MRS CHANDLER. I'm so glad you could come.

KERSHAW. Coffee, Sarah?

MRS CHANDLER. Yes, I'd love some, please. (KERSHAW *pours some coffee.*) Oh Peter, I'm sorry, do you know Frank Kershaw?

CROSBY. Yes, of course I know Frank.

MRS CHANDLER. Central Office very sweetly sent him up to represent the party.

KERSHAW. That's not quite true, Peter. Dozens of them wanted to come, but your aunt insisted that she wanted it kept as small as possible. (*He gives* MRS CHANDLER *her coffee.*)

MRS CHANDLER. Thank you, Frank.

Pause.

Do you know if they've arrived?

PLATT *coughs.*

CROSBY. Oh, I'm sorry. Frank, this is Jim Platt, foreman, isn't it?

PLATT. Works Manager.

CROSBY. Sorry, works manager at Baron Castings, local foundry. And more importantly, constituency chairman. Jim, this is Frank Kershaw, whose many commercial concerns are too numerous to mention.

PLATT. Oh, yes, we all know Mr Kershaw.

KERSHAW. I didn't know my fame had spread so far.

MRS CHANDLER. There, you see, Frank —

PLATT. Cos, actually, we're one of his numerous concerns.

Pause.

CROSBY. Small world.

KERSHAW. What did you say your —

PLATT. Baron Castings.

KERSHAW. Oh, yes, of course.

Slight pause.

You're doing rather well, aren't you?

PLATT. Well, that's not quite correct, Mr Kershaw. It'd be a bit more accurate to say we're doing rather badly.

Pause.

CROSBY. No-one's doing well, after all.

Slight pause.

KERSHAW. See the trade figs, Peter?

CROSBY. I did. Of course, a lot of it's still oil . . .

KERSHAW. That doesn't mean we don't have to pay it.

CROSBY. Roll on the North Sea, say I.

KERSHAW. As soon as Mr Wedgwood Benn rolls off it . . .

PLATT (*breaks in, as a joke*). Oh for the days of Empire, eh, Peter? Send in the gunboats, sort the Saudies out that way.

CROSBY (*smiles*). The sun will never set, eh, Jim? Last for a thousand years?

MRS CHANDLER. There was something to be said for it.

CROSBY, *taken aback by her tone, looks to* KERSHAW, *who nods at the portrait.*

CROSBY. Oh, I'm sorry, I didn't mean —

MRS CHANDLER. It's all right, Peter. Of course, I know it's changed. The nation, and, indeed, the Party. Once we stood for patriotism, Empire. Now it's all sharp young men with coloured shirts and cockney accents, reading the Economist. We stand or fall, how capable we are. Perhaps, however, not inspiring — quite . . .

Pause.

KERSHAW. I think I heard the car —

MRS CHANDLER. You should hear Peter, Frank. He's really very witty. Especially when they talk about the Dunkirk Spirit. Says we must be the only nation in the world that's inspired by battles it lost.

CROSBY. I'm sorry.

MRS CHANDLER. Are you going to stand?

CROSBY. Stand?

MRS CHANDLER. For the candidacy.

CROSBY (*carefully*). I had thought of it. But it's entirely up to you.

MRS CHANDLER. I'd be delighted.

A knock. KERSHAW *goes and speaks to someone outside.*

CROSBY. Really?

MRS CHANDLER. Really.

KERSHAW. They're ready, Sarah.

MRS CHANDLER. Off we go, then.

Exit KERSHAW *and* MRS CHANDLER.

PLATT. Look, Peter, if you'd rather not bother today, after the funeral, and that . . .

CROSBY. No, it's fine.

PLATT. Another day, if you prefer . . .

CROSBY. No, it's fine.

PLATT *goes.* CROSBY *looks at the portrait.*

You old bastard. You're laughing at me.

Blackout.

Scene Three

In the darkness, the voice of a young Brummie, PAUL.

PAUL. Bob! Hey, Bob!

Lights. The bar of the Labour Club. A table, on it three pints and an ashtray. Stools. CLIFTON *and* SANDY *are playing darts. He's in his early 30s, dressed in an oldish corduroy suit and tie. She's perhaps a little younger, from the North, neatly dressed in denim.*

CLIFTON (*throws a dart, then*). Paul!

PAUL *appears. Mid-20s, wearing jeans, denim jacket, open-necked shirt, carries a rolled-up piece of paper.*

PAUL. Bob, I think we done it.

CLIFTON (*marking up his score*). How d'you work that out?

PAUL. Well, get a load of this.

SANDY *throws as* PAUL *makes a space on the table and spreads out his piece of paper. We see it's a map, with sections coloured in. He weighs down the chart with the ashtray and a glass.* SANDY *marks up and comes over.*

CLIFTON. That pint's yours. Hey, have you met Sandy?

PAUL. No. How d'you do?

SANDY. Hallo.

CLIFTON (*going to the board and throwing*). Paul's in charge of getting me the nomination, darling. He thinks I'm a bit fuzzy on Clause Four, but he's backing me because of the opposition. He's what the Express calls an unrepresentative, militant minority. He started reading Tribune at the age of two, he hates Roy Jenkins just a little more than Adolf Hitler, and Reg Prentice gets apoplexy at his very name. (*Coming back to the table.*) But what he doesn't know about the Labour Party Rulebook isn't there. That's right?

PAUL. That's right.

CLIFTON. Now.

SANDY *to throw, as.*

PAUL. Right. Calculations as follows. 40 union delegates eligible. And on my estimate, them as turns up breaks circa 50/50. And odds and sods like women, YS and the Co-op, all for you. OK?

CLIFTON. Fine.

SANDY (*returning*). Yours, Bob.

CLIFTON. 'Scuse I.

CLIFTON *to throw,* SANDY *looks at the chart.*

SANDY. That looks very impressive.

PAUL. It's just a matter, know the rules.

SANDY. And then, exploit them?

PAUL. Use.

CLIFTON (*returning*). OK.

He sits, indicating a suspension of the game. SANDY *sits.*

PAUL (*pointing at the chart*). Right. So the key's the wards. That's over half the delegates. Now, right-wing wards, the ones you lost already, marked in pink. That's Greenside and Fenley Heath. The reds you got, no bother: Grimley and Broughton Park. The floaters, Stourford and West Thawston, see?

CLIFTON. I see.

SANDY. D'you think, the other feller, what's his name —

PAUL. John Smalley? Not a chance.

SANDY. Not even — as an ex-MP?

PAUL. Especially, as an ex-MP. (*He takes a xerox sheet from his pocket. To* CLIFTON.) Now, as it happens, neither of the floaters got their full quota of ward delegates for the General Management Committee. In Thawston, nothing like. And they can nominate from now until they fix election day. And so — the strategy — recruit new members like there's no tomorrow, pack the GMC with folk'll vote for you, it's in the bag. OK?

CLIFTON. Won't Smalley too?

PAUL. He'll try. But here's the point. Cos obviously, them two, we're talking of our pals from overseas. And, as it happens, on that, Mr Smalley's got his drawers in something of a tangle.

He waves the xerox. SANDY *comes over to them.*

Hansard, Parliamentary Report. Second reading, Kenya Asians Bill, Feb 1968. The Hon. John Smalley, then MP for Sheffield East. I quote. (*He reads.*) "Whatever one's sympathies — and I have many — with these unfortunate people, one must accept that the indigenous population will not for ever stay silent, faced with what appears to be the thin end of a very thick black wedge."

CLIFTON. He said that?

PAUL. There in black and . . . well, you know.

CLIFTON. That's great.

PAUL. We do it as a leaflet. Bung it round. We got him by the plums, Bob. Like a jerbil in a bucket.

CLIFTON *goes to throw.*

SANDY. So what about the Tory?

PAUL. Eh?

SANDY. You got Bob candidated, or whatever. What about the Tory?

PAUL. Well . . . (*Confidentially, to both.*) The Tory. Two in it, so I hear, like us. On one hand, Chandler's nephew, chap called Peter Crosby. You know, bright, high-flier, all slim suits and unit trusts. The other, something altogether different.

CLIFTON. Well?

PAUL. One Major Rolfe. Wild man, with eagle eye. Who thinks the Carlton Club is in the pay of Moscow, and would put himself just slightly to the Right of Ghenghis Khan.

CLIFTON. He's possible?

PAUL. Who knows? With that lot. Does it matter, anyroad? (*He picks up his pint.*) Whatever, come the day, it's hallo Robert Clifton, honourable member.

CLIFTON *raises his glass.* SANDY *follows suit.*

I give you, comrades — the Collapse of Capital.

PAUL *and* CLIFTON *clink and drink.* SANDY *sips her beer. Blackout.*

Scene Four

Lights. Empty set. ROLFE, *now in his mid-50s, stands centre. He wears a black overcoat, with medals, and a poppy.*

ROLFE. In '47. Came on home.
Major Rolfe. A face of stone.
Another England, seedy, drab,
Locked in the dreams of glories she once had.
The Major looks at England and bemoans her tragic fate,
Condemns the mindless comforts of a flaccid, spongers' state,
Despairs of trendy idiocies repeated as a rote,
While the knot of old school tiredness is still tight round England's throat.
Sees leaders fat with falsehood as they lick up every lie,
The people's blood grown sickly with their driving will to die.
Major Rolfe, sees the light,
Calls for a counter from the Right:
Major Rolfe, starboard seer,
Loses, for they will not hear.

Enter KERSHAW, *dressed similarly to* ROLFE.

KERSHAW. Lewis.

ROLFE. Frank.

KERSHAW. How are you?

ROLFE. Fine. And you?

KERSHAW. I'm fine.

Pause.

How's the boy?

ROLFE. Alan? He's fine too. Just got promotion. Captain.

KERSHAW. Splendid.

ROLFE. Sails for Belfast on the midnight tide.

KERSHAW. That's fine?

ROLFE. Arrives in time to see the dawn rising over Ballymurphy.

KERSHAW. Breathtaking.

ROLFE. Indeed.

Pause.

KERSHAW. And business?

ROLFE. Brisk. And yours?

KERSHAW *shrugs, smiling.*

I didn't get the candidacy, Frank.

KERSHAW. What?

ROLFE. Do you remember? I was going for the Tory nomination, Taddley.

KERSHAW. Oh, yes –

ROLFE. Didn't have a chance, of course.

KERSHAW. Oh, surely, I thought by now you're due for –

ROLFE. Up against the perfect opposition.

Slight pause.

KERSHAW (*smiling*). Well, go on.

ROLFE. Oh, Frank, he looked just right. Knew all the right words, too – concerned, humane, constructive, moderate . . . With just the right note of apology in his voice when he had to admit to being a Conservative as well . . .

KERSHAW (*slightly embarrassed*). Bitter.

ROLFE. Perhaps. His hatred of privilege, you see, doesn't stop him showing off his stripy tie.

KERSHAW. In fact, I know him, Peter Crosby. Nephew of a friend of mine.

ROLFE. So then you'll understand.

Pause.

What's it matter, anyway? The state the Party's in.

KERSHAW. What state is that?

ROLFE. Self-loathing. Gutless. Genuflecting to the fashionable myths.

KERSHAW (*with some irony*). What myths might they be, Lewis?

ROLFE. Oh, the full employment myth, the ever-rising wages myth, the higher public spending myth, the whole social-democratic demonology of workers good and bosses bad, all those myths . . .

KERSHAW. Now, surely, Lewis. All that's changed. I read my Daily Teleg-

ROLFE (*interrupts*). Oh, yes, we'll say, the Party's changed, at last we've understood, we have the Right Approach, and yes, of course, at Party conference, our new and True-Blue leaders, to a person, bang the drum and flap the flag . . . It's just, you see, we learn from history, in practice, come the crunch, the flag they wave omits the red and blue.

Pause.

KERSHAW. What's the alternative?

ROLFE. That is the question.

Slight pause.

KERSHAW. OK, Lewis. I've got the message. Brimstone and hellfire. So, how must we be saved?

ROLFE. There's a group of us have lunch from time to time.

KERSHAW. That's nice.

ROLFE. To talk about what happens after.

KERSHAW. What happens after lunch?

ROLFE. What happens when the river breaks its banks.

KERSHAW, *perhaps deliberately, not understanding.*

The cold Class War hots up.

KERSHAW. Oh, Lewis, surely not.

ROLFE. Not what?

KERSHAW. Not Suffolk military geriatrics, drilling private armies on their croquet lawns.

ROLFE. Of course not. There's no need for private armies.

KERSHAW. Well, exactly —

ROLFE. When, already, we've a public one.

   Slight pause.

   One of our little group is Alan's Brigadier.

   Pause.

KERSHAW. You're seriously suggesting — army into Government?

   ROLFE *shrugs.*

   In England?

ROLFE. All right. What happens? Wage control collapses, unemployed take over factories, council tenants massively refuse to pay their rents, in name or not, another General Strike, the pound falls through the floor, the English pound, the English river's burst its English banks . . . So what d'you do? You either let the deluge, deluge, or you build a dam against it. Mm?

   Slight pause.

   We've got to think about it, Frank —

KERSHAW. Wasn't it R.A. Butler said — politics, the Art of What Is Possible.

ROLFE. No. It wasn't.

KERSHAW. Oh, I'm sure it —

ROLFE. Butler borrowed it. From Bismarck.

   Pause.

KERSHAW. Why talk to me?

ROLFE. I'm testing water.

KERSHAW. Only mine?

ROLFE. No, any Managing Director of a major British company whose shares were two pounds fifty eighteen months ago and at the close on Friday just topped sixty-four.

   Pause. KERSHAW *brusque.*

KERSHAW. No, Lewis.

ROLFE. No? Why not.

KERSHAW. Can't see it in those terms.

ROLFE. Won't see it.

KERSHAW. Still have some faith in people's reason.

ROLFE. Reason? Your shop stewards, reasonable men?

KERSHAW. In people's loyalty.

ROLFE. To what?

KERSHAW. The national interest.

ROLFE. Whose? Whose loyalty? The miners? Students? Irish? Blacks?

KERSHAW. Lewis, there's no need —

ROLFE. And whose interest, hm? You talk of our national interest, and they listen? Come on, Frank. They know which side they're on. And so should we.

KERSHAW. The dogmas of class war . . .

ROLFE. Yes, yes. And why?

KERSHAW. Tell me.

ROLFE. Because if we turn craven, we collaborate, we are betraying people who, if they're not on our side, are left in no-man's land, ripe for defection. The NCO's. The lower-middle-class.

KERSHAW. Yes, well?

ROLFE. Who, on all counts, have been betrayed. Their property no longer secure. Their social status, now, irrelevant. And in the place of what's important to them, national destiny and hope, we've given them . . . You see, Frank, it's not true that we've lost an Empire, haven't found a role. We have a role. As Europe's whipping boy. The one who's far worse off than you are. Kind of — awful warning system of the West. And to play that role, we must become more shoddy, threadbare, second-rate. Not even charming, quite unloveable. And for those — the people that I come from, that despair is a betrayal.

Enter DENNIS TURNER, *stands upstage. He is nearly 50, dressed soberly, wears a poppy, carries a wreath.* KERSHAW *and* ROLFE, *sensing the ceremony is about to start, move to stand upright, together.* ROLFE *quietly, to* KERSHAW.

And if they go, we've lost. And go they will, unless they feel defended. So for them we must arm the national interest. Fortify it. Build the dam, for them.

Pause. A VOICE.

VOICE. Let us commemorate and commend to the loving

memory of our Heavenly Father, the shepherd of souls, the giver of life everlasting, those who have died in war for our country and its cause.

'They shall grow not old, as we that are left grow old. Age shall not weary them, nor the years condemn. At the going down of the sun, and in the morning, we will remember them.'

RESPONSE (TURNER, ROLFE *and* KERSHAW). We will remember them.

A very long silence. TURNER *lays the wreath. The Last Post is played on a bugle. As it finishes.*

VOICE. The Legion of the Living salutes the Legion of the Dead.

RESPONSE. We will not break faith with ye.

KERSHAW *speaks quietly to* ROLFE.

KERSHAW. Maybe.

Blackout. KERSHAW *and* ROLFE *go.*

Scene Five

Immediately, a spot hits TURNER.

TURNER. In '47. Came on home.
    Sergeant Turner, to a Midlands town.
    Another England, brash and bold,
    A new world, brave and bright and cold.
    The Sergeant looks at England, and it's changed
        before his eyes;
    Old virtues, thrift and prudence, are increasingly
        despised;
    Old values are devalued as the currency inflates,
    Old certainties are scoffed at by the new
        sophisticates:
    And big capital and labour wield an ever-bigger clout,
    And it's him that's in the middle and it's him that's
        losing out —
    Sergeant Turner, NCO:
    Where's he going? Doesn't know.

Full lights. TURNER's *Antique shop. 1970 Election Conservative Party posters on the wall: Vote Conservative for a Better Tomorrow. Enter* TONY, *blonde, late teens, and* PAUL, *a few years younger than when we last saw him. They carry an antique table.*

TONY. Turner's Antiques. Employee: Tony Perrins. Like the work. And learn a trade. Investment for the future.

PAUL. Turner's Antiques. Employee: Paul McShane. Dislike the work. But, out of school, job market bleak, just take what you can get.

They set the table and go out.

TURNER. Selling old things. Beautiful things. Heavy with craft.

Enter PAUL and TONY with two antique chairs.

TONY. Years ago. June, 1970. Election results. Labour lost. Pollsters confounded. Gaffer's pleased.

PAUL. Years ago. June, 1970. Election results. Tories won. Lame ducks and rising unemployment. Selsdon Men. A Black Day.

They set the chairs either side of the table. TONY *takes* TURNER's *overcoat from him, goes out and re-enters, as:*

TURNER. An end to six years of socialist misrule. At last, the little man will get his chance against the big battalions.

Enter MONTY, about 30, Jewish, cockney accent, long hair, brushed denim suit, open-necked shirt. He carries a union jack carrier-bag and smokes a thin cigar. To TONY:

MONTY. 'Morning, flower. See the boss?

TONY. Someone to see you, Mr Turner.

TURNER *looks to* MONTY. *Some distaste.*

MONTY. Good morning, Mr Turner. Montague Goodman. New neighbour. Thought it time we had a chat.

Slight pause.

Just call me Monty.

TURNER. Neighbour.

MONTY. That's correct. We are developing next door.

TONY. Look of surprise, the gaffer's face.

PAUL. Horror, more like.

Exit TONY and PAUL.

TURNER (*sits*). Developing next door to what?

MONTY (*sits*). A shop.

TURNER. I hadn't heard.

MONTY. So hence our chat.

TURNER. What kind of shop? It might affect my trade.

MONTY. It will, old love. Antiques.

Pause.

TURNER. What d'you mean, antiques?

MONTY. Selling old things. Beautiful things. Heavy with
nostalgia.

TURNER (*stands*). Who are you?

MONTY. Didn't I present my card? (*He stands, gives* TURNER
his card. Out front.) I told him to ignore the company. It
being what you might call defunct.

TURNER. You what?

MONTY (*out front*). Quite elegant, the system, as it happens.
Buy a name, in our case several, firms that've stopped trading
but still have listed Boards and all that stuff . . . And in that
name you go to an estate agent, in our case several, and buy
a series of adjacent properties, separately of course, complete
the deals, wind up the firm.

TURNER (*sits*). I don't get what you mean.

MONTY (*out front*). So told him. Idea was to conceal a whole
row being bought by one developer. And, naturally, that
developer's identity. But nothing he could do, and liked his
face, so told him. (*Sits, to* TURNER:) That you, Dennis
Turner, are now a tenant of the Metropolitan Investment
Trust.

TURNER. You what?

MONTY. They've sold the building, love.

TURNER. Who has?

MONTY. Your landlord.

TURNER. But —

MONTY (*out front*). Though, truth be told, he put up quite a
fight. (*He stands and walks about.*) In fact, eventually, we had
to ring the council, do a bit of bartering. Luckily, we found
they were but bursting to erect a SupaParkarama down the
road, needing to demolish a pair of properties at that time
in our gift. So we said, look, old chums, you don't want
all the fuss of buying us out, why not slap a CPO on number
27, grounds of rot, and we can call it quits. Well then, of
course, we told his landlord, purchase order on its way, you

couldn't see his signature for dust. Wouldn't even have matched our offer, see.

TURNER. What's happening to my shop?

MONTY (*out front*). I told him, plan was for a precinct, geared towards the younger end. Boutiques, hair stylists, soda fountains, drive-in legal aid facilities, antique emporia, self-service massage parlours, all that kind of thing. (*To* TURNER:) And this particular retailing zone is pencilled in as a zen macrobiotic luncheon take-away, old love.

TURNER. You're joking. I've got a 12 year lease.

MONTY *sits, picks up his union jack bag, plonks it on the table, takes out a document, as he speaks.*

MONTY. Now there you are correct. Unfortunately the law, in that majestic way it has, does give a little leeway. Quote: the rent is subject to a periodical review. Sunbeam, you have just been periodically reviewed. Direction: up.

TURNER. You can't do that.

MONTY. Now there you're incorrect.

TURNER. I'll pay it. I'll refuse to go.

MONTY. Oh, petal, please.

TURNER. Why shouldn't I?

MONTY (*out front*). I hate this bit. (*He stands, facing away from* TURNER.) Tulip, I don't know if you've noticed, but among the merry navvies labouring next door are several of our Caribbean cousins. Simple, cheery folk, all charmers to a man, but tending to the slapdash. Natural exuberance, you see. The kind of natural exuberance that pushes bits of scaffolding through windows, picking off the Georgian porcelain.

Pause. He neatly stubs his cigar out on the table top.

TURNER. You bastard.

MONTY (*back to the table, putting the document back in his bag*). No, not bastard. Selsdon man.

TURNER. But why destroy my livelihood.

MONTY (*harsh, quick, nearly angry*). Because, my love, destroying you will make someone somewhere some money. All it is. Cupidity. What you got, but just not enough. Cos we, we make our money out of money. We covet on a global scale. We got cupidity beyond your wildest dreams of avarice. And you, the little man, the honest trader, know your basic handicap? You're suffering a gross deficiency of greed. (*Briskly, as he goes:*) You've got three weeks, old love.

MONTY *goes. Pause. Enter* TONY *and* PAUL, *either side.*

TONY. We came in. Saw the gaffer. Shattered.

TURNER. Lunch, you two.

PAUL. It wasn't half past twelve.

TONY. We told him so.

TURNER. I said, it's lunch.

PAUL. We went.

PAUL *goes. Pause.* TURNER *waves* TONY *out.* TONY *goes.* TURNER *stands, looks at the table and the stubbed-out cigar.*

TURNER. So where do I go now.

Blackout.

Scene Six

Lights on an upstairs pub room. The date is 20 April, 1968. Tables, chairs. On a table an old Grundig tape-recorder. An easel, with a picture on it, covered in a red cloth. MAXWELL, *a thin, neat man in his early twenties, is finishing the distribution of the chairs.*
Then enter CLEAVER, *mid-fifties, distinguished, and* DRUMONT, *a middle-aged French Canadian, who carries a glass of scotch, and has a raincoat over his arm.*

CLEAVER. Thanks very much, David.

MAXWELL *nods and goes.*

Well?

DRUMONT (*tossing his coat over a chair*). Looking good, Richard.

CLEAVER. We think so.

DRUMONT. Whole world over. Detroit to Grosvenor Square. Particularly here. The sell-out blatant. Deeper rot. Unthinkable ideas beginning to be thought. What an opportunity.

CLEAVER. Indeed.

DRUMONT. I would be so confident, Richard, but for one factor.

CLEAVER. Which is?

DRUMONT. You. The revolutionary movement. The essential vanguard. Where are you, Richard?

CLEAVER. Edward, you know . . .

DRUMONT. No, Richard, no. I'll tell you where you're at. You're stuck in 1930. You're still fighting old battles, tearing yourselves apart with petty sectarian squabbles that you should have settled years ago.

CLEAVER. Edward, the reason why — (*A knock. Impatiently:*) Yes?

Enter MAXWELL.

MAXWELL. I think everyone's here now. They're in the bar, and they're wondering . . .

CLEAVER (*looks at his watch*). Oh, yes, of course, tell them to come up. (MAXWELL *goes. To* DRUMONT:) The will is there. It's money.

DRUMONT. When the movement in Britain demonstrates that it is seriously committed to unity, then money follows. Simple.

CLEAVER. We're having talks —

DRUMONT. On unity?

CLEAVER. That's right.

DRUMONT. Then see that they're concluded.

CLEAVER. Yes. Of course.

DRUMONT. Richard. It's nineteen hundred and sixty-eight. Student riots. Workers striking. Chaos and decay. In ten years time, where could you be? I tell you. Out of the cellars, Richard. Out of the basements and into the sun.

A knock.

CLEAVER. Come in.

The door opens and a number of PARTYGOERS *enter. In the main, young. Most have drinks. Some greet* CLEAVER. MAXWELL *is with them.* DRUMONT *picks up his coat to go.* CLEAVER *to him.*

CLEAVER. You going?

DRUMONT. I want an empty ritual, I go to church. So — au revoir.

CLEAVER. Goodbye.

DRUMONT goes. MAXWELL to CLEAVER.

MAXWELL. Who was that?

CLEAVER. Edward Drumont. Canadian. The man with all the money.

MAXWELL. And?

Slight pause. CLEAVER shrugs.

CLEAVER. Let's get the formalities over with.

MAXWELL and CLEAVER move to the centre. MAXWELL bangs a glass for silence. During his speech, the PARTYGOERS group round, some sitting.

MAXWELL. Comrades. If I could have your attention. Comrades. It's my pleasure to ask Dick Cleaver, on behalf of the movement, on this very special day, the 20th of April 1968, to propose the toast of fealty.

Applause. During CLEAVER's speech, MAXWELL takes a tray of candles from below a table, and lights them.

CLEAVER. Thank you. Comrades, I'm not going to make a long speech . . .

SOMEONE. That'll be the day!

Laughter. CLEAVER smiles.

CLEAVER. Though I do believe that a good speech should be like a woman's skirt: short enough to arouse interest, but long enough to cover the subject. (*Laughter.*) Anyway, all I really want to say is how good it is to see a group of people like this, particularly the young ones, in this day and age . . . (*Laughter.*) You probably know, you probably saw in Grosvenor Square last month, a lot of today's students are attracted to communism as an alternative to the evils of the capitalist system. And they're right. It is an alternative. Under capitalism, man is exploited by man. Under communism, it's precisely the other way round. (*Laughter.*) But we know that, don't we. Anyway.

SOMEONE. That's cos you told it last year!

CLEAVER (*smiling, good humoured still*). And there's more where that came from! No, just the one, I promise. There's these two Jewish businessmen on a train. And they're discussing ethics. And one says — I tell you a story that illustrates perfectly the problem of ethics already. Here am I in this shop I run with my partner Hymie. And this man comes in for his suit. And I give it him and I say that is £10 and he gives me the money. But when he has gone I find he has given me by mistake £20 already. So here as I say I have the ultimate ethical problem. Do I, or do I not, tell my partner.

Laughter. Suddenly, serious.

But I don't have to tell anyone here about that kind of ethic. Or the degeneracy of youth today. Or how our beloved country is being deliberately destroyed. I needn't tell you that. You've got your noses. You can smell the stink.

Slight pause. Jovial again.

Well, that's my lot. So, without further ado, can I ask you to raise your glasses and join with me in toasting the memory of the man whose birthday we have come together to celebrate. David —

The PARTYGOERS *take candles from the tray.* SOMEONE *switches off the light, leaving the scene candle-lit.* MAXWELL *takes the curtaining off the picture. It is Adolf Hitler.*

The Fuehrer.

ALL (*raising their glasses*). The Fuehrer.

MAXWELL *switches on the tape recorder. A German recording of the SS marching song, the Horst Wessell Lied. The* PARTYGOERS *take off their jackets. Some are wearing armbands, showing the sunwheel symbol; others put on armbands, badges, flashes. By small additions to basically black, brown and blue costumes, their ordinary clothes become uniforms. As each* PARTYGOER *finishes changing, they salute the portrait, and go and stand by the tape recorder, joining in the song, with English words.* CLEAVER *is the last to salute the picture of the Fuehrer.*

SONG.   We march and fight, to death or on to victory,
         Our might is right, no traitor shall prevail
         Our hearts are steeled against the fiery gates of hell
         No shot or shell can still our mighty song.

> Our sword is truth, our shield is faith and honour,
> In age or youth, our hearts and minds we pledge,
> Though we may die to save our people and our land
> This course will stand, our millions marching on.

A knocking starts at the door. The song peters out.

> We close our ranks, in loyalty and courage,
> To God our thanks, for comrades tried and true . . .

MAXWELL (*switching off tape recorder*). Who is it?

DRUMONT (*off*). Drumont.

CLEAVER. Let him in.

SOMEONE *puts the light back on. The feeling of panic in the group subsides.* MAXWELL *admits* DRUMONT, *who carries a folded newspaper. He stands, says nothing.*

CLEAVER. Yes, Edward?

DRUMONT *hands the folded paper to* CLEAVER.

DRUMONT. Read that.

CLEAVER. What is it?

DRUMONT. Evening paper. Read. From there.

CLEAVER. What is it?

DRUMONT. Read.

CLEAVER (*upset at being ordered about, nonetheless starts to read*). 'A week or two ago I fell into conversation with a constituent, a middle-aged, quite ordinary working man employed in one of our nationalised industries. After a sentence or two about the weather, he suddenly said: "If I had the money to go, I wouldn't stay in this country". I made some deprecatory reply, to the effect that even this government wouldn't last for ever' . . . . (*He looks to* DRUMONT.)

DRUMONT. Well, go on.

CLEAVER. . . . 'but he took no notice, and continued: "I have three children, all of them have been through grammar school, and two of them married now, with family. I shan't be satisfied till I have seen them all settled overseas. In this country in fifteen or twenty years time the black man will have the whip-hand over the white man".' (*He looks up.*) Edward, who is —

DRUMONT (*takes the paper, turns it over, points*). Now, there. Read on.

CLEAVER. 'The cloud no bigger than a man's hand, that can so rapidly overcast the sky, has been visible recently in Wolverhampton and has shown signs of spreading quickly. As I look ahead, I am filled with foreboding. Like the Roman, I seem to see . . . (*Slight pause.*) "The River Tiber foaming with much blood".'

Pause.

All right. Who is it.

DRUMONT. The Right Hon Enoch Powell, Shadow Spokesman on Defence. Saying what no-one but you has ever dared to say. (*Pause. He lets it sink in. Then to* MAXWELL.)

You a tough guy, soldier?

MAXWELL. I like to think so, sir.

DRUMONT. This hurt? (*He hits* MAXWELL *suddenly in the stomach.* MAXWELL *flinches slightly, shakes his head.*) OK, now take off that stuff.

MAXWELL. I'm sorry, sir?

DRUMONT. Shirt, armband. All that fancy dress.

MAXWELL *looks to* CLEAVER, *who shrugs a nod.*
MAXWELL *takes off his shirt and armband. Again, suddenly,* DRUMONT *hits him.*

Hurt any more? The second time?

MAXWELL. No, sir.

DRUMONT. That's good. (*He turns to the rest of the* PARTY-GOERS.) Right. Comrades. For years, you have been battering against a bolted door. (*He waves the paper.*) And now, it's open. You can join, and build, and move. To do so, you must spurn the trappings. Spurn the fripperies. But not the faith. Not, absolutely not, the faith. (*He walks around,* ALL *watching him.*) For as you grow, you will, of course, be faced with heresies. Two heresies. And rather easy to define. Beware the man — the Right Conservative, the disillusioned military man — who'd take the Socialism out of National Socialism. But, also, even more, beware the man — the passionate young man, the Siegfried — who would take the National out of National Socialism. Guard against them both. Keep strong. Keep faith. And keep your long knives sharp. (*He covers the*

Hitler portrait with the curtaining.) And so. Not always. For a time. (*He tosses the newspaper to* MAXWELL *as he goes.*)

Pause.

CLEAVER. Where was he speaking?

MAXWELL (*looks at the paper*). Birmingham.

Pause.

CLEAVER. Rivers of blood.

The scene freezes, and LIGHTS *cross-cut to a spot on* KHERA, *at the side. He's now in his early forties, bareheaded, short-haired, clean shaven. He wears the protective clothing of a foundry worker, and carries his mask and goggles in his hand.*

KHERA. In '58. Came on home.
      Gurjeet Singh Khera. To a Midlands town.
      Another England, another nation,
      Not the England of imagination.
      The labour market forces have an international will,
      So the peasants of the Punjab people factory and mill,
      The sacred kess and kanga, kachka, kara and kirpan
      The Sikh rejects so he can be a proper Englishman;
      Keep faith in human virtue, while attempting to
          condone
      The mother country's horror at her children coming
          home.
      Gurjeet Singh Khera,
      Once a slave,
      Returns to haunt the Empire's grave.

PLATT (*off*). Khera! Khera! For Christ's sake, Khera, where the bloody hell you hiding?

PLATT enters into a little light on the other side of the stage. He's in a dirty white coat, carries a clipboard. Pause.

KHERA. Sir?

Blackout. Play Handel.

ACT TWO

'The rise of the Nazi Movement signifies the nation's protest against a state refusing the right to work . . . protest against economic order thinking only in terms of profit and dividends.'

Gregor Strasser, National
Socialist Reichstag Deputy,
10 May 1932

'It is because we want socialism that we are anti-semitic.'

Joseph Goebbels, 1931

'The term socialism in itself is unfortunate, but it is essential to realise that it does not mean businesses must be socialised . . . This sharing of the workers in possession and control is simply Marxism.'

Adolf Hitler,
22 May 1930

'Only an anti-semite is a true anti-communist.'

Adolf Hitler, 1931

Act Two

Scene One

Lights. PLATT *and* KHERA *in the same positions. Noise of machines. The* CHARACTERS *have to shout,* PLATT *rather more than necessary.*

PLATT. OK. Now what's all this I hear.

> PATEL *enters. Dressed the same as* KHERA, *stands near him. About 25.*

KHERA. About?

PLATT. About your people banning overtime.

KHERA. It's not decided yet. We'll let you know. (*He turns to go.*)

PLATT. No good, mate. In your contracts. 28 a month.

PATEL. It's also in our contract you speed up the track?

PLATT. Nothing against it, bab.

PATEL. And chargers, casters, knock-out men, no increased pay for increased work?

PLATT. You're not on piecework, mate.

PATEL. Unlike the moulders.

PLATT (*angry*). Oh, for Christ's sake —

KHERA (*quietly*), And, obviously, coincidence that all the moulders white.

PLATT. Look, mate. It's not my fault, all Asians on fixed rates. Not my fault, all the moulders white. You ought to see your union.

KHERA. We are our union. (PATEL *and* KHERA *turn to go.*)

PLATT (*shouts after them*). Cos I don't give a toss, you're black, white, brown, or pink with purple stripes. As long as you keep working, don't —

PATEL. Precisely, Mr Platt.

PLATT (*shouts after* KHERA). Well, Mr Khera?

KHERA (*turns back*). As shop steward, I have called a meeting. Let you know.

PLATT, *angry, leaves.* PATEL *shakes his head, half-smiling at* KHERA, *and goes out.*

KHERA (*out front*). The Foundry industry. Long hours. Hot, dangerous conditions. Asians lowest paid, least chances of promotion, first to go.

ATTWOOD, *white foundryman, but ordinary clothes, crosses the stage, giving no acknowledgement of* KHERA, *and goes off.*

(*Sardonically.*) And taking British workers' jobs away.

He goes, as blackout.

Scene Two

Lights. A meeting hall. Table at the back, on a raised platform. Microphone. PEOPLE *at the meeting include* TONY, *longer-haired than in Act One, with a guitar under his seat;* MRS HOWARD, *an elderly gentleperson; and* LIZ, *lower middle-class, late 20s. Various other* PEOPLE. TURNER *is making heavy weather of pinning up a banner:* TADDLEY PATRIOTIC LEAGUE. *On the banner, somewhere, is a union jack.* MAXWELL *enters. He is now nearly 30, slim suit, tastefully fashionable. He taps* TURNER *on the shoulder. All the dialogue until the meeting proper is unprojected, part of hubbub of general conversation. During it,* ATTWOOD *enters, and sits.*

TURNER. Oh, hallo David. Nearly ready for the off.

MAXWELL. Fine. Just rung Cleaver. Think it's go.

TURNER. That's great.

MAXWELL *sits.* TURNER'*s task is complete.* TONY *goes over to him quickly, as if he's been waiting to catch him.*

TONY. Um, Mr Turner —

TURNER (*looks at his watch*). Yes, Tony?

TONY. You won't forget the poem, will you?

TURNER. Poem? Oh, no, of course not.

TONY *grins, sits.* TURNER *to himself, as he goes behind the table.*

Right.

MAXWELL *suddenly stands, and goes over to him.*

MAXWELL. Oh, Dennis.

TURNER. Ar?

MAXWELL. Just one thing, I noticed. On the banner.

TURNER. Ar?

MAXWELL. You've got the flag the wrong way round.

TURNER (*coming round to look at the banner*). Oh, blimey, have I?

MAXWELL (*smiling*). Doesn't matter. Sadly no-one notices. But, p'raps, for next time . . .

TURNER. Sure.

He grins at MAXWELL. MAXWELL *smiles back, and sits again.* TURNER *behind the table again. He speaks through the mike, which feeds back.*

Good evening ladies and gentle — Oh God. (*He adjusts the mike. It still feeds back.*) Good evening, ladies — (*Away from the mike, he calls.*) Could we, is there anyone in the box? (*Pause. Grins.*) Technological miracle. (*Pause. This time, the mike's dead.*) Testing, testing. Now we've lost it altogether. Testing, test — (*Amplification in.*) — ing, testing. Ah. One, two, three, four. That's better. Ladies and gentlemen, as I was saying before being so rudely interrupted, good evening to you all. Now I've called this meeting, as most of you know, to discuss two things, both of which are related to each other. One is the forthcoming bye-election, in Taddley, and the other is the possibility of the Patriotic League joining forces with a national organisation. And with this in mind, we have here tonight Mr Maxwell, who's leader, is that right, David?

MAXWELL. General Secretary.

TURNER. Sorry, general secretary of the Nation Forward party, a truly patriotic organisation as I'm sure you'll all agree when you've heard what he's got to say. First of all, though, there is the question of paying for the room, and I wonder if someone —

LIZ. I'll do it, Mr Chairman.

TURNER. Oh, thanks, love.

LIZ goes round collecting.

Always collect before the speaker, eh? Now, first of all, I hope you've all seen the new bulletin. If any of you a'n't, we've got a great new system which might not quite work yet.

Anyway, I've got a spare or two. (*He picks up a bulletin.*)
Now, we've gone as far as we dare on some of this. I don't
mind what the Race Relations people say, but the printers get
a bit jumpy. Anyway, one thing I would like to draw your
eye to is on page four, the item about parasitic worms at
Thawston Junior, cos I did write to the Medical Officer of
Health about it. I think he's getting a bit fed up with me,
actually. Perhaps eventually he'll get fed up enough to do
something about these immigrant problems in our schools.
Anyway, he wrote back in his usual soothing vein, I hope
some time he'll realise that the patriotic people of Taddley
can't be soothed that easily. One of the things I said was that
the thing about these parasitic complaints is that they're
passed on by cutlery and using the same toilet. Of course
that's when these people sit on the toilet. Usually they do
other things as you know. Anyway, he didn't say much about
that in his reply. Anyway, there was just that one point I
wanted to point out before I handed over to Mr Maxwell
to explain to us all about Nation Forward. Thank you.

He sits, polite applause. MAXWELL *goes behind the table,*
TURNER *adjusts the mike for him.*

MAXWELL. I think, actually, I'll dispense with the electronic
aid. (*Not into the mike.*) In fact, I thought, despite Mr
Turner's splendid build-up, that I wouldn't launch off into a
great diatribe, I think you all know something about Nation
Forward, and I think it'd be a lot more useful if we threw
the discussion open now, so that you can ask the questions
you want answering, and, most importantly, that I can listen
to what *you* have to say.

He sits. Pause.

TURNER. Well, that's stunned 'em all into silence, Mr Maxwell.

MAXWELL *smiles. Pause.*

Come on, I'm sure somebody —

Pause. To fill in.

Well, I think one thing people might want to ask is —

MRS HOWARD *stands and interrupts. During all
contributions,* MAXWELL *takes notes.*

MRS HOWARD. Mr Chairman.

TURNER. Ah, Mrs Howard. I thought you'd find voice sooner
or later.

MRS HOWARD. Mr Chairman, I have been a member of the Conservative Party for 40 years. That's what I wish to say.

Pause. TURNER starts to ask her if that's it.

TURNER. Is that, er —

MRS HOWARD *(interrupts)*. It would be complete anathema to me to support or vote for any other party.

Pause. Again:

TURNER. Are you saying —

MRS HOWARD *(interrupts)*. However. I am afraid that the Party is not what once it was. It has become craven. Once it represented all the finest values of the middle class. Now, gangrenous.

Pause. Again:

TURNER. Yes, well, I'm —

MRS HOWARD *(interrupts)*. Values sneered at. Sniggered over. In the Party. The Young Conservatives, who often seem more socialist than the socialists themselves. They look embarrassed, when you talk about the Empire, or self-help, or discipline. They snigger, talk about the Common Market. Sneer, and talk about a wind of change.

Longer pause.

TURNER. Mrs Howar —

MRS HOWARD *(interrupts)*. I'm sure it's infiltrated. From the left. The cryptos. Pale-pinks. Sure of it.

Pause. TURNER does not interrupt.

I recall it, you will understand, as once it was. That's all I have to say. *(She sits.)*

MAXWELL. Mrs Howard, could I say that yours is exactly our view.

LIZ *(stands)*. Mr Chairman, I'd like to say something. I'm sure what the lady says is true, but it's not just politics. My husband — he can't be here tonight — he lectures at the Poly. And he's become convinced of several things. One is that half these so-called foreign students aren't studying at all. They turn up once, then disappear. And, also, he's quite sure at least 75 per cent of the lecturers, and some of them are immigrant, are communists. And cos of this, he may lose his job. Cos he's a patriotic person, and makes no secret of it, when they cut back, and they're going to, he'll be the first to go. The union won't lift a finger. And another thing. It's folk like us, who work for Britain, who are suffering the most. Like when they talk about home ownership, the Tories in particular. What happens? Mortgages go up so far we can't afford the payments. So we say, OK, we'll sell. But even that's impossible. Our house is in West Thawston, and you know, you say that you're from Thawston and they all start talking pidgin English. So we can't sell. Or buy. So people get desperate. Really desperate. There seems no way, you see. (*She sits. Pause.*)

TURNER. Anyone else?

MRS HOWARD (*stands*). In my opinion —

TURNER. Mrs Howard, if anyone else wants —

MRS HOWARD. Just one point, Mr Chairman. Following on what the young lady said.

TURNER (*shrugs*). The floor is yours.

During this, ATTWOOD *is growing irritated.*

MRS HOWARD. In my opinion, the lady is quite right. It is the silent majority who are suffering. In silence. As they watch their green and pleasant land become more and more like an Asian colony. And the do-gooders. Isn't it time, Mr Chairman, that we thought about the victims for a change? And hasn't the tide of permissiveness, the erosion of old values, gone too far? That's what they're saying. The people on fixed incomes. With inflation. No big unions protecting them. What about the people without a union. What about us?

ATTWOOD *stands and interrupts.* TURNER *whispers his name to* MAXWELL. *After a few moments,* MRS HOWARD *sits.*

ATTWOOD. Look, Mrs, let me tell you something. I reckon I'm patriotic as you are, but I'm in a union, and I've voted Labour all my life, and I'll tell you what's bothering me. I'm in motors, steward in a foundry, and what concerns me, with the business like it is, is that if it's a British firm it's going bankrupt, and if it's American, some great Detroit tycoon picks up his phone and says, more profit if we shift the lot to Dusseldorf. And there's summat else. Cos what jobs there are we're not going to get. I doubt if you know Baron Castings, where I work, but come dinnertime there's that many turbans in the canteen, it

looks like a field of bloody lillies. And smells like the Black
Hole of Calcutta. And if one of 'em gets the push, they're all
up in arms, shrieking about discrimination. It's happening
now. And I'll be quite frank about the blacks, I hate 'em. And
no-one's doing bugger all about it. That's what bothers me.
Not the erosion of your bleeding middle-class values. (*He sits.*)
Sooner or later, summat's got to be done. (*Angry, to* MRS
HOWARD.) So don't you talk to me.

Tense pause. TONY *stands.*

TONY. Er, Mr Chairman —

TURNER. Tony?

TONY. I think, what the last speaker was saying. You know, I
mean, you're middle class, and you lost your business, didn't
you, I hope you don't mind me saying, but I mean it was the
same, big firm taking over . . . And take me. I'm on the dole,
in' I? Like you were saying. It just does seem to me, what
class you are . . . same, kind of . . .

He's run out. MAXWELL *stands.* TONY *sits, relieved.*

MAXWELL. If I could perhaps come in there. Well, my friends,
I said I thought I'd learn a thing or two from you, and by
God was I right. We've heard about subversion in the colleges.
From Mrs Howard about the Tory Party. And from Mr —
(*Checks a note.*) Attwood on the local industry. But it's my
view that the last speaker really grasped the point. That what
we have in common is greater by far, than what divides us.
I'm sure, for instance, that Mrs Howard does not oppose
trade unions as such, but only their perversion for political
ends. I am convinced that Mr Attwood does not oppose
honest profit, but speculative profiteering. Of course, we
disagree on many issues. But more, much more, unites us than
divides us. It's an old saying, but you can change your class
and your creed. But you can't change the blood in your veins.

The odd 'Hear hear'. MAXWELL *smiles.*

But I'm afraid we've something else in common here. To use
a light-hearted phrase, we all feel 'Fings ain't what they used
to be'. More seriously, we all of us observe a gradual decay,
disintegration, in our fortunes and the fortunes of our nation.
And perhaps there is a reason — that we have a common enemy.

Oh, of course, it looks like many, different enemies — to the
young lady it's the college reds, to Mr Attwood it's the multi-

nationals, to Mrs Howard it's the banks who recklessly
promote inflation and destroy her savings. And it's called by
many names — names representing things we're taught to see
as opposites — socialism, liberalism, communism, finance
capital. Things that, in fact, aren't opposites at all.

You know, there are those who still laugh when we talk
about conspiracy. Even when we look at those people who are
promoting immigration. Even when we look at those supposed
guardians of free enterprise who talk about detente and sell
their grain to bolster Bolshevism. There are people, still, who
laugh at the idea of a conspiracy. A world-wide conspiracy.

But there's one, small group of men and women who don't
laugh. There is one, small, growing party which knows what
is happening and is determined to reverse it. That is Nation
Forward. And I hope, with all sincerity, that you will wish
to join this party, join with us, and make our country great
again.

Pause. He sits.

TURNER. Well, follow that. I think we'd best move straight to
a vote. Um — that the Taddley Patriotic League henceforth
is amalgamated within and serves as a branch of the Nation
Forward Party. I think that does it. All in favour?

All except ATTWOOD *vote. Pause.* ATTWOOD *votes.*

Nem. con.

MAXWELL. I think I can say on behalf of the whole movement
how delighted I am at this decision.

TURNER. Thank you, Mr Maxwell, I'm sure we —

MAXWELL (*interrupts, smiling*). I *can't* say, on behalf of the
movement, anything specific about the bye-election yet, but
we are hoping to stand, and my personal view is that there
could be no more suitable candidate than your Chairman,
Dennis Turner.

Applause.

TURNER (*pleased but taken aback*). Well, David, I don't know
what to say . . . I think anyway we better call it a night . . .

TONY *puts his hand up.*

If there's nothing else —

TONY. Mr Turner —

TURNER. Oh, I'm sorry. One other item. Tony Perrins, here, with a fine show of initiative, he's written a patriotic song, and I'm sure it'd be a very fitting epilogue to such a good meeting. Come on, bab, let's have you.

TONY, *nervous, stands, picks up his guitar, goes to the platform.*

(*To* MAXWELL.) I think, move into the stalls, eh, David? (MAXWELL *and* TURNER *move and sit in the body of the hall.*)

TONY (*sits on the edge of the table, takes his guitar out of its case*). It's — I didn't write the words, it's a poem, I just set it to music — (*He strikes a chord, to check the tuning, and breaks a string.*) String gone. Won't take me a second. (*It does. Some shuffling of feet.*) That's it. Um — The Beginnings. By Rudyard Kipling, 1914. Set to music by Anthony Perrins. (*He has a little cough. Then sings. At first not very well, unsure, but growing increasingly assured, harsher, building to the climax.*)

It was not part of their blood
It came to them very late
With long arrears to make good
When the English began to hate

They were not easily moved
They were icy willing to wait
Till every count should be proved
'Ere the English began to hate

Their voices were even and low
Their eyes were level and straight
There was neither sign nor show
When the English began to hate

It was not preached to the crowd
It was not taught by the state
No man spoke it aloud
When the English began to hate

It was not suddenly bred
It will not swiftly abate
Through the chill years ahead
When time shall count from the date
That the English began to hate.

A grin.

That's it.

Blackout. In the darkness, to cover the change, we hear the message of a car loudspeaker.

MAXWELL'S VOICE. People of Taddley. This is Nation Forward, the party which puts Britain first. Our nation is under threat. The scourge of unemployment still ravages. Working people are made to suffer for the mistakes of corrupt politicians, while property sharks and speculators live off the fat of the land. Most of all, treacherous politicians have conspired to flood our country with the refuse of the slums Africa and Asia. Vote for a change. Vote Nation Forward. Vote Dennis Turner.

The tape fades.

Scene Three

Lights. The Labour Club. CLIFTON and SANDY with drinks. PAUL with KHERA, in a suit, and PATEL, in casual clothes.

PAUL. Gurjeet Khera, Prakash Patel; Bob Clifton, Sandy Clifton.

KHERA. How d'you do.

SANDY. Hallo.

CLIFTON (*brisk, but not aggressive*). Right. So what d'you want?

KHERA. We wondered, Mr Clifton, if you knew about the Baron Castings situation.

CLIFTON. Yuh. In part.

KHERA. And if, well, you could —

PATEL. We want support.

CLIFTON. Go on.

PATEL. We gave you ours. We voted for you, delegates from Thawston, and gave you our support. Now we want yours.

CLIFTON. I see. So could you, for the detail, fill me in? "

PAUL. Well, Bob, as I was saying —

CLIFTON. Not you, Paul.

KHERA (*aiding himself with notes*). Well. The dispute at Barons began as a conflict over retimed jobs, required a higher workload for the same reward. And as only unskilled workers don't receive a bonus, and as most are Asian, this job retiming is itself discriminatory. But also this had highlighted discrimination in promotion, whereby high-paid moulders' jobs have gone exclusively to whites. Because of this, the unskilled workers, after due negotiation, have imposed a ban on overtime.

Pause.

CLIFTON. Yuh. Go on.

KHERA (*not using the notes as he grows in confidence*). There is a union, Association of Diecasters and Foundrymen. In fact, within the foundry, it was we who built the union. Now, for five weeks, we have fought, banned overtime, without assistance. We have passed motions, sent letters, proceeded through the correct channels. Even when dismissal notices were served on us, they did nothing.

CLIFTON. So —

KHERA. We occupied their offices.

SANDY. The union?

KHERA. That's right.

CLIFTON. And then?

PAUL. They've made the ban official.

CLIFTON. Good. So what's the problem?

PATEL. So, the ban on overtime's official. On a piece of paper. Registered at Congress House, wherever. Doesn't mean, for moulders, it's official.

CLIFTON. No, of course.

PATEL. And with a racist party, in the bye-election. Making propaganda. Leafletting. And so on.

CLIFTON. Yes.

Pause.

OK. It's clear discrimination. Ban's official. Legal. So I'll make a statement. Backing your dispute. OK?

KHERA *is about to reply when* PATEL *stops him with a gesture.* CLIFTON *notices.*

Problem?

PATEL. Question.

CLIFTON. Shoot.

PATEL. What's in all this for you?

CLIFTON. Why do you ask?

PATEL. We don't have that much reason to have faith in Labour
— any British politicians.

CLIFTON. No, you don't. The answer to your question's
nothing. It doesn't gain me anything at all, to swim against the
tide. So, why? Don't know. Tell me.

Slight pause.

KHERA. Thank you.

CLIFTON. Not at all.

KHERA, PATEL *and* PAUL *go,* PAUL *giving* CLIFTON
a thumb's up sign.

CLIFTON (*to* SANDY). Members.

SANDY. I beg your pardon?

CLIFTON. That's what he meant. D'you remember. Paul's
recruiting drive in Thawston? In a sense, they got me
nominated.

SANDY. Ah. I see.

CLIFTON. Not that it's — I mean, I would have backed them
anyway.

SANDY. Oh, sure. Bob?

CLIFTON. Yuh?

SANDY. What are you apologising for?

Slight pause.

CLIFTON. Dunno.

Blackout. In the darkness, another car loudspeaker message.

TURNER'S VOICE. People of Taddley. This is Nation Forward,
the party which puts Britain first. Our nation is under threat.
The scourge of inflation still ravages. Independent businessmen are being squeezed out by punitive taxation while social
security scroungers live off the fat of the land. Most of all,
treacherous politicians have conspired to flood our country
with the refuse of the slums of Africa and Asia. Vote for a
change. Vote Nation Forward. Vote Dennis Turner.

Fades.

Scene Four

Nation Forward Campaign HQ. Tables, chairs, typewriters. Too much paper, too little space. LIZ is sitting at a table, addressing envelopes.
Two doors: one, with a spyhole, leads into the street; the other to an inner room.
Bell. LIZ stands, checks through the spyhole, admits TONY and TURNER. They both wear union jack rosettes.

TURNER. Hallo, Liz. Mr Maxwell about?

LIZ. He's in the back. Said you'd want to see this. Evening Post. (*She gives him a newspaper.*)

TURNER (*sits*). Oh, ta.

LIZ. Coffee?

TURNER. That'd be lovely.

LIZ. Tony, could you —

TONY. Sure. (TONY *sits, addresses envelopes.* LIZ *goes into the inner room.* TURNER *laughs.*) What is it, Mr Turner?

TURNER. The Labour candidate. Bathering on about this nig dispute at Barons. Gonna get his prick caught in his zip, he don't watch out. (TONY *smiles. Enter* MAXWELL *from inner room.*)

MAXWELL. Hallo, Dennis. Seen the story?

TURNER. Ar, I have. And the Tory's not much better.

MAXWELL. What? No, I meant our statement on the immigrant voters. Page three, top of.

TURNER (*turns page*). Oh, ar?

LIZ *enters with a tray of coffees.*

LIZ. David?

MAXWELL. Liz, you're a treasure.

TURNER (*taking a cup as he reads*). Ta. (LIZ *gives* TONY *a cup, sits with her own, addresses envelopes, as:*) This is good stuff, David.

MAXWELL. I think it'll capture the initiative.

TURNER. Got to be right.

MAXWELL. By the way, did you manage to glance through the draft election address?

TURNER (*puts down the paper, finds a typescript in his pocket*). Oh, yuh.

MAXWELL. Any worries?

TURNER. Well, yes, actually. One or two.

MAXWELL (*sits*). Shoot.

TURNER. Now, you'll laugh at this, but I found some of it a bit left-wing.

MAXWELL (*smiles*). In what way?

TURNER. Well, a lot of it's great — all the stuff on the nigs, law and order, you know — red hot. But this business about import controls and nationalising banks, I mean — you know what I mean?

MAXWELL. Not exactly.

TURNER. I'm not sure how it'll go down.

MAXWELL. With Tory voters.

TURNER. Yes.

MAXWELL. But we're not just after Tory voters.

TURNER. Well, no. But there's stuff in here about opposing wage controls —

MAXWELL (*slightly impatient*). Of course we are opposed to wage controls. (*Pleasant again:*) Only insofar as we believe that the crisis is created by ruthless international speculators, and that it should not be paid for by the British working class. You see?

TURNER. Well, still —

MAXWELL (*stands*). That's good.

TURNER. And there's the parasitic worms.

MAXWELL. I beg your pardon?

TURNER. The Medical Officer's report on parasitic worms among immigrant schoolchildren.

MAXWELL. Well, yes, I did think, best to keep it fairly general . . .

TURNER. But it proves what I been saying all along.

MAXWELL. Yes, surely but I do think, we've got some general statistics —

TURNER (*stands*). But this is bloody dynamite —

MAXWELL (*patiently*). Look, Dennis. We're not — we can't be, just a pressure group, on any issue, even one as central as the colour question. We're a party, and as such, face other parties whose ideologies are total, all-encompassing. We too must, therefore, show we have a comprehensive view. We are not, merely, hard-line patriots. We are not, certainly, ersatz Conservatives with a particular distaste for immigration. We are British Nationalists, with a cogent and distinct world-picture of our own. You see?

TURNER. I don't think you know them round here.

Pause. Bell. LIZ goes to answer the door as:

MAXWELL. All right. All right. I'll bow to your superior local knowledge. We'll insert a specific reference.

LIZ *checks, admits* CLEAVER. *He is slightly older than when we last saw him.*

CLEAVER. Ah. Splendid. Veritable hive.

MAXWELL *nods hallo.*

TURNER. Afternoon, Richard.

CLEAVER. Soldiering on, Tony? How's it going.

TONY. Fine, thank you, sir.

CLEAVER. Splendid. Keep it up. (*To* TURNER *and* MAXWELL.) Mulling over the address?

MAXWELL. That's right.

CLEAVER (*taking the typescript*). Any problems?

MAXWELL. Dennis was worried about some of the economic stuff. Living standards. Banks.

CLEAVER (*leafing through*). That's right?

MAXWELL. I pointed out the need to pose a definite alternative to the bankrupt policies of the old parties.

CLEAVER (*still leafing*). That's good.

MAXWELL. Particularly, that we should dissociate ourselves completely from backwoods Conservative elitism.

CLEAVER. Of course. You see, Dennis, unlike the Tories, we are not unconditional supporters of the economic status quo. Specifically, we oppose the spivs and parasites of credit or financial capital. At the same time, of course, as seeking to eliminate the Marxist wreckers in the factories. Indeed, our view is that financial capital and communist subversion are, in essence, just two pincers of the same conspiracy to undermine the nation's enterprise.

TURNER. It doesn't say that here.

CLEAVER. So it would seem.

Pause.

Dennis, why don't you and Elizabeth go and map out the visiting.

TURNER. Right.

LIZ *and* TURNER *go into the inner room.* CLEAVER *still reading,* TONY *listening as he works.*

MAXWELL. Jesus Christ.

CLEAVER. What's the matter?

MAXWELL. Turner's obsession with disease.

CLEAVER. I didn't know he had one.

MAXWELL. He has, for starters, a positive paranoia about parasitic worms.

CLEAVER. Parasitic whats?

MAXWELL. Worms.

CLEAVER. David, I'm not totally happy with this.

MAXWELL. Well, it's got to be at the printers by tonight.

CLEAVER. Oh, it's just a few omissions. Tony, go and see if Mr Turner wants a hand.

TONY. Yes, sir.

Exit TONY *into the inner room.*

MAXWELL. Well?

CLEAVER. Well. (*He reads:*) 'Nation Forward believes that the cause of our present crisis is not the legitimate wage demands of British workers, but the domination of our economy by a tiny clique of international capitalists — the very people who deliberately import cheap foreign labour and cheap foreign goods to undercut our wages and to throw us on the dole.'

Pause.

MAXWELL. Well?

CLEAVER. Drop the wog-bashing and it could be Tribune, David.

MAXWELL. So what d'you want? Wicked unions holding the country to ransom? Eastbourne über alles? Cos that's what Turner —

CLEAVER (*angry, stabbing at the typescript*). Where, amongst all this jolly stuff on the thieves' den of the Stock Exchange, is the support of free productive industry? Where, amid all this merry rhetoric about the plight of ordinary working-folk, is the need to isolate the Commie wreckers? Where, in the midst of all this happy talk of democratic structures and meaningful participation, is the hint, no more, the hint that all men are not equal and that some were born to lead and others only fit to follow?

MAXWELL. Richard, we can reprint Mein Kampf if it'll make you —

CLEAVER. David, I am liable to lose my temper —

MAXWELL. Richard, I've had Turner down my throat all afternoon. I am trying to run a campaign from a disorderly shoebox staffed by juvenile mental defectives and to be frank I couldn't give a toss about your temper.

Pause.

CLEAVER (*icy calm, ripping up the typescript as he speaks*). Were it not, David, for the boundless charity of those of us who, against all the evidence, saw behind your gauche facade the faintest glimpses of potential, you would still be in your army surplus pants and scout-hat goose-stepping up and down in Epping Forest, or, perhaps, organising Nordic Kulturfests on Clapham Common, or, perhaps, being sent down for laughable offences like attempting to arrest the Premier for treason, or, perhaps — (MAXWELL, *furious, takes a wild swing at* CLEAVER, *who catches his wrist.*) Well done, David. For a moment, then, you ceased to look neanderthal. Almost, a prepossessing specimen. For once.

Bell. CLEAVER *and* MAXWELL *still locked. Bell again.* CLEAVER *releases* MAXWELL, *who sits, furiously, and engages immediately in busy activity as* LIZ *enters, goes to the door and checks through the spyhole.*

LIZ. I don't know who it is.

CLEAVER *looks through the spy-hole.*

CLEAVER. Oh, now this is a surprise. Go and fetch Mr Turner, Elizabeth. He has a visitor.

LIZ *exits.* CLEAVER *admits* CROSBY, *who carries a newspaper.*

Good afternoon, Mr Crosby. My name is Cleaver. And this is David Maxwell.

CROSBY. Dennis Turner in?

CLEAVER. Just coming. Do sit down.

CROSBY *sits.*

I read your statement in the Post today.

CROSBY. Oh, yes?

CLEAVER. Do tell me, is it sexual?

CROSBY. What.

CLEAVER. This kick you get from batting for the other side.

Pause.

Nice for you, though. Uncle kicks his boots off, you step in.

CROSBY *is about to reply, when* TURNER *comes in.*

TURNER. Oh, Mr Crosby. To what do we owe —

CROSBY (*stands, gestures with the paper*). Mr Turner, I've just been studying your plans to sabotage this bye-election.

TURNER. Sabotage?

CROSBY. I've come to ask you to reconsider your plans to harass immigrant voters. Quote: 'We do intend to monitor all immigrants who in our view aren't bona fide voters, during this election, at the Polling Stations.' Well?

TURNER. Oh, after the nig-vote, are we?

CROSBY. I — have most unwillingly come.

TURNER. Look, you know as well as I do, half of them's not entitled, and the other half votes twice.

CROSBY. Will you reconsider?

TURNER. Will I hell.

CROSBY. Then I shall report you to the Returning Officer.

TURNER. You do that.

Pause.

CROSBY (*angry*). There's no need, you know, to make the whole thing mucky, drag us all . . . No need, but I suppose it's all part of your national regeneration, using these Gestapo tactics — Oh, I'm sorry. You'd probably view that as praise. These — red Bolshie bully-boy tactics then. (*He turns to go.*)

MAXWELL. We'd have the reds any day, Mr Crosby. Blood in their veins. Our most committed people, working-class ex-reds.

CROSBY. Oh, I'm sure you recruit from various lunatic fringes, not just the one.

MAXWELL. Better to be extremely right than extremely wrong.

CROSBY (*going to the door*). What a fatuous remark, can't you do better than that?

CLEAVER. Mr Crosby, I have an uncle —

CROSBY. How nice. Mine's dead. Goodbye, Mr Turner —

CLEAVER. — who lives in Southall. Never been involved in politics. Probably votes Labour. And this harmless old fellow is quite genuinely terrified that after he's dead, some time in the future, an Indian temple may be built over his grave. Which may seem absurd, and, what's the jargon, paranoic to you. And it might seem very passé, very old-fashioned, very unhip to say that that old boy did not fight in two world wars to die, for whatever reason, an unhappy, lonely, terrified old man.

Pause. CROSBY *is completely thrown.*

CROSBY. I think . . . I think I . . . I don't think there's any more can usefully be said.
He goes.

CLEAVER (*briskly, as he goes to the inner room*). You see what we mean, Dennis? Feeble. Flabby. Like all Tories, a slave to sentiment.

He's gone. TURNER *looks at* MAXWELL. MAXWELL *a wry smile as blackout and a spot hits* CROSBY, *one side of the stage, and* PLATT *on the other.*

CROSBY (*to* PLATT). And it was very strange, when talking to these people; thought, oh, no, these can't be, with their grisly xenophobia, they can't, or are they, our creation, Demons. Alter-ego. Somehow. (PLATT *smiles.*) And I remembered, being small, the Coronation, and the climbing of Mount Everest, a kind of homely patriotism, sort of, harmless, slightly precious self-content. A dainty, water-colour world, you know. (PLATT *looks embarrassed.*) And then, their monstrous chauvinism. Dark, desire, for something . . . Kind of, something dark and nasty in the soul.

Pause. PLATT *has a little cough.*

Felt out of time.

PLATT. Beg pardon? Out of what?

CROSBY. I'm scared.

Blackout.

Scene Five

During the following, fade up lights. PLATT *is still there.* KERSHAW, *in an overcoat and with an overnight case, comes in to him.*

VOICE. This is Taddley. This is Taddley. The train just arrived at platform two is the 15.57 from Birmingham New St, forming the 16.18 to West Bromwich, Dudley, Bilston and Wolverhampton. Platform two for the 16.18, all stations to Wolverhampton.

PLATT *hands* KERSHAW *a thick file.* KERSHAW *opens it, then looks back to* PLATT.

KERSHAW. Look, words of one, Jim. What they after?

PLATT. Extended bonuses. An end to so-called promotional discrimination.

KERSHAW. Can we concede the latter, ditch the former?

PLATT. No chance. Whites won't wear it.

KERSHAW. Why?

PLATT. No cash in it for them.

KERSHAW. And giving them the lot?

PLATT. You'd still have bother, now.

KERSHAW. I see. We'll have to break it, then.

PLATT. Or allow it to break us.

KERSHAW (*looks at* PLATT). Jim, you do understand, why I'm here.

PLATT. Not really. Very small dispute.

KERSHAW. It was. While they were banning overtime.

PLATT. Now, look, that's not my fault. That's bloody union.
They said they'd back the ban. They let the whites work
normal, didn't they. No wonder that our sunburned brethren
lost their rag. Not my fault, that they're coming out on strike.

KERSHAW. Not my fault, sadly true, that with no manifolds or
brake-drums, can't make motor-cars.

Slight pause.

PLATT. Think that's called the hyper-mutuality of capital-
intensive high technology.

Slight pause.

According to my lad's Financial Times.

Slight pause.

KERSHAW. So. Can the police do nothing?

PLATT. They say no.

KERSHAW. Why not?

PLATT. They can. But won't.

KERSHAW. But come on, Jim, an unofficial strike —

PLATT. You tell the good Inspector. (KERSHAW *looks at*
PLATT.) You can see their point. The cameras, press, and
all. It's tough for them, politically.

KERSHAW. Can see my point? Three plants, dead stop. Tough,
economically, for us.

PLATT. I see. I think that's called a contradiction.

KERSHAW. Jim, for heaven's sake . . .

Pause.

PLATT. I know a young man. Who's in something of a crisis. He
decided, 'bout a week ago, he couldn't cope with being a
Conservative. Which wouldn't matter if he wasn't standing for
election as a Tory in four days. We all have problems.

KERSHAW. Yes.

Pause.

Remind me, the percentage. Black to white.

PLATT. 'Bout six to one.

KERSHAW. Bad odds.

PLATT. What for?

KERSHAW. The picket line.

Pause.

D'you know if Nation Forward know about the strike?

PLATT. Why ask?

Slight pause.

KERSHAW *(suddenly, briskly, walking out.)* An English river, brimming English banks. *(He has gone.)*

PLATT. I don't get what you mean.

Blackout.

Scene Six

In the darkness, on a cassette tape recorder, TURNER practising a speech. He's not doing it well. During this recording, lights fade up on Nation Forward's HQ, evening. CLEAVER and MAXWELL sit. LIZ and TONY — who has the tape recorder near him — are working on a banner upstage. TURNER is standing behind a chair, which he'll use as a lectern.

TURNER *(on tape)*. And p'raps most of all, you'll hear the Left. You'll hear them call us Fascists. And, far worse — for as we know for them, for as we know for them, you're to the Right of — who's this?

MAXWELL *(on tape, at a distance)*. Trotsky.

TURNER *(on tape)*. Trotsky you're a Fascist, you'll hear them claim that we, the British Nationalists, are nothing more than tools of business and the ruling order, and, that if in power . . . sorry?

MAXWELL *(on tape, at a distance)*. And that, if in power . . .

TURNER *(on tape)*. Sorry, can I start again?

MAXWELL *gestures to* TONY, *who switches off the tape recorder.* TURNER *smiles, shrugs.*

MAXWELL. OK, let's leave that. Try some questions.

Slight pause. CLEAVER *asks the first question.*

CLEAVER. Mr Turner, would you admit to racial prejudice?

TURNER. We all have a natural and healthy preference for our own kind.

MAXWELL. Colour?

TURNER. That's what I mean. Certainly, giving an Asian a British passport doesn't make him British.

MAXWELL (*prompting*). Cat.

TURNER (*rushing slightly, as if a line learnt by heart*). After all, just because a cat is born in a kipper box, it doesn't make it a kipper.

LIZ *and* TONY *look up, react to the joke.* CLEAVER *looks at* MAXWELL.

And have you heard the one about —

CLEAVER (*interrupts*). Turner, there's pressure from the Pakkies for a separate girls' school, religious grounds. Approve?

TURNER. All for it. As long as it's in Pakistan.

CLEAVER. No!

TURNER. Why not? It's funny.

CLEAVER. Flip. You say it shows the immigrants themselves can't integrate.

TURNER (*shrugs*). Ask me another.

MAXWELL. Repatriation.

CLEAVER *holds up three fingers.*

TURNER. Ordered . . . compassionate . . . humane. (*He stops.* CLEAVER *gestures him on.*) But we are honest enough to say that it cannot be voluntary. And that includes all immigrants who were born here.

CLEAVER. No!

TURNER. What's wrong?

CLEAVER. How on earth can an immigrant be born here? Remote control?

TURNER. Well, you know what —

CLEAVER. That's exactly what the hecklers want.

MAXWELL. And on the same score, Dennis, don't say they breed like rabbits.

TURNER. Why?

MAXWELL. Cos then some joker shouts that Queen Victoria did too.

Pause. CLEAVER *looks at* MAXWELL.

CLEAVER. All right. This strike at Barons.

TURNER. The main priority must be — to resist, present attempts to secure a backstairs deal, between the immigrants and the company, um — above, uh —

MAXWELL. Over the heads —

TURNER. Over the heads of the British workers.

MAXWELL. A deal which once again would prove —

TURNER. Would prove —

MAXWELL. The common interest —

TURNER. Of the multi-nationals and the multi-racial elements in our midst.

MAXWELL. So?

TURNER. So, naturally, in the event of management reneging on the interests of the ordinary white workers, we must show our support.

MAXWELL. No, Dennis, no. In the event of management *selling out* the interests of the *rank and file* white workers we must *demonstrate* our *solidarity*.

TURNER. Oh, ar. That's right. I'm sorry.

CLEAVER *looks at* MAXWELL. MAXWELL, *rather self-satisfied, stands and goes to look at* LIZ's *work over her shoulder.* CLEAVER *leans back in his chair.*

CLEAVER. Mr Turner, I wonder, could you tell us just a little more about this common interest, between the multi-nationals and the blacks?

TURNER. Well, it's them attracts them. Them as advertised in all the papers over there. And when they're here, it's them — the multi-nationals — who encourage them to so-called integrate.

CLEAVER. I see. Now why would they do that?

MAXWELL (*still looking at* LIZ *and* TONY's *work*). Wages.

TURNER. Yuh, to undercut the wages of white workers.

CLEAVER. Only wages?

MAXWELL (*still looking at the work*). Jobs.

TURNER. That's right, to take jobs that would normally be given to the whites.

CLEAVER. No more than that?

MAXWELL *looks at* CLEAVER.

Nothing to do with — make-up? Breeding? And the aim, perhaps, to mongrelize . . .

TURNER. You what?

CLEAVER. To turn our nation to a mongrel race of khaki half-castes . . .

TURNER. Ar, and that as well.

MAXWELL (*walks back to* TURNER *and* CLEAVER, *firmly*). Come on, Turner, you're just Fascists in sheep's clothing. Look at Cleaver's Nazi record!

CLEAVER (*scratching his ear*). Look at Maxwell's.

MAXWELL. You're just tinpot Führers, out to overthrow democracy!

TURNER. That's not —

MAXWELL. Come on! Question! Answer it! (*He sits.*)

TURNER. If you'll just let me. There's a simple answer. We want more democracy. We think that at the moment we're controlled by an undemocratic, cosmopolitan elite of Wall Street — puppeteers — who are behind the plot to undermine the nations, the free nations, and impose a One-World State, which would be under their control. Their methods include — strangulation of the national economies by saddling them with debt . . . and, (*Looks to* CLEAVER.) and mongrelisation, and communist subversion, and — (*He looks at* MAXWELL.) the creation of the multi-national monopolies.

MAXWELL. Well done.

TURNER (*during this speech,* CLEAVER *starts laughing, long and loud*). In its place, we wish to build — a truly democratic . . . nationalist society, in which the views, of everyone, are — as it were . . . What's funny?

CLEAVER (*laughing*). Oh dear me.

TURNER (*quite angry*). What's funny?

CLEAVER. Wall Street? In alliance with the Communists? Oh dear me.

TURNER. Well, they financed the Russian Revolution —

CLEAVER (*laughing even more*). Financed the Russian

Revolution? New York bankers? Oh, that's good, that is.

TURNER. Well, it's been said —

CLEAVER (*still jovial*). I mean, for heaven's sake. Name names.

TURNER. Well, Jacob — Schiff, and Otto . . .

MAXWELL. Warburg.

TURNER. Warburg, they gave cash to pay the Bolsheviks to —

CLEAVER (*laughing even more*). Schiff and Warburg? Oh, that's rich, that is. That's really rich. I mean, now, what on earth had they in common with the Communists? Just tell me. What on earth?

Pause. Still smiling.

Just tell me. What on earth. In common.

Pause.

TURNER. Richard, I don't get —

CLEAVER (*not smiling any more*). Or put another way. What British landlords. British tenants. British workers. British bosses. Have in common.

TURNER (*quietly*). Race.

CLEAVER. Can't hear.

TURNER. Their race.

CLEAVER. And so — the others?

Pause.

Warburg. Marx. Schiff. Rosa Luxemburg. Rothschild. Lev Davidovitch Trotsky. What have they in common.

TURNER. Richard, I'm not an anti-sem— (*He stops himself. Pause.*)

CLEAVER. Dennis. The man who took your shop away. What was his name?

Pause.

TURNER. Goodman. Monty Goodman.

CLEAVER. Yes.

The telephone rings. CLEAVER *answers it.*

Yes? Oh, yes, indeed. Hold on.

He covers the receiver.

And so the questioner's remark about democracy. What is democracy?

TURNER. What serves. Is in the interests of. The Race.

CLEAVER (*stands, walks towards the exit, carrying the telephone on its long lead*). That's right. (*To* MAXWELL.) Goodnight, David. (*He turns at the exit, gestures with the receiver to* TURNER.) It's for you.

CLEAVER *goes out with the telephone.* TURNER *shrugs at* MAXWELL, *follows.* TONY, *his work done, stands, sits on a chair.* LIZ *looks up at* MAXWELL.

MAXWELL. Well?

LIZ. Well what?

MAXWELL. Can't you see what he's doing?

LIZ. Who?

MAXWELL. Herr Obserstgruppenführer?

LIZ *goes back to her work.*

LIZ. Tell me.

MAXWELL. You know, he has this vision of himself, he really sees himself in cap and flashes, striding through Earls Court or somewhere, flanked by cohorts of the brightest and the blondest . . .

Slight pause.

You see, Liz, what he'll never realize, you can't, now, operate a show on Nordic runes and Wagner, there's some people out there going to need convincing, and we must appear . . .

Slight pause.

I mean, OK, the Triumph of the Will, but not just his . . .

TONY. Don't matter what we say, as long as we get votes, that what you mean?

MAXWELL (*drops into a chair*). Oh, blimey. What's the point.

LIZ, *her work done, stands. She takes out a cigarette.*

LIZ. I like things neat.

She lights her cigarette.

I used to do a lot of sewing. Not just clothes, but things around the house. The curtains, chair covers. I even did a bit of tapestry, picked it up at school. The house was getting really nice. But then, with everything, there didn't seem much point.

There was this tenants' group, a lot of them, in fact, were Patriotic League, you know, the thing that Dennis ran. And what was good about it wasn't that they said the things I thought, but that, with them, I could express myself, without apologising.

Why shouldn't I? Why shouldn't I be proud of what I am? Our country's rotting. Fabric's perished. Ripping at the seams. Cos people won't be proud of what they are. I don't care how it comes about. I want a reason to have children.

TONY. Yuh. That's right.

Enter CLEAVER.

MAXWELL. Well, who was that on the —

LIZ (*interrupts*). Banner's finished, Richard.

CLEAVER. Let me see.

TONY *and* LIZ *lift up the banner. A union jack, behind an* appliqué *white family. The slogan: 'The Future Belongs To Us'.*

Yes, that's very good.

Slight pause.

MAXWELL (*suddenly, almost desperately*). Oh, for Christ's sake, Tony, told you, hundred times, the top left white band's broader, look, you got the thing the bloody wrong way round —

TONY. I'm not the only one.

Pause. CLEAVER, *as if noticing* MAXWELL *for the first time since he came back in.*

CLEAVER. Oh, David. You still here?

Pause.

Tony, get Mr Maxwell's coat.

MAXWELL. I haven't got a coat.

CLEAVER. Tony, get Mr Maxwell out of here.

TONY *goes to* MAXWELL. TURNER *has entered, he watches the scene.*

MAXWELL. Look, I . . . Tony, look, you —

TONY. Heard what Mr Cleaver said?

MAXWELL. Oh, God Almighty.

He turns and quickly exits. TONY *gestures at the banner.*

CLEAVER. It doesn't matter, Tony. Been a long night. (*He sits.*)

'TURNER. What's happening? Why's David gone?

CLEAVER (*patiently*). Dennis. There is, in Nationalist politics, a heresy, it's more or less perennial, which argues that true patriots should be opposed, not just to international finance, but to private enterprise in toto. And what follows? An obsession with 'democracy'. Masses, as against the individual. Distrust of leadership. Marx, decked out in patriotic weeds.

Pause.

We've had a little purge.

Slight pause. Briskly.

Right. Once more. The speech.

Blackout.

Scene Seven

Immediately, spot on TURNER, *in front of the banner. If possible, he should be radio-miked. His speech is cool, assured, professional. It echoes round the theatre.*

TURNER. And p'raps most of all, you'll hear the Left. You'll hear them call us Fascists. And, far worse — for, as we know, for them, you're to the Right of Trotsky, you're a Fascist — you'll hear them claim that we, the British Nationalists are nothing more than tools of business and the ruling order; and that, if in power, we'd destroy the democratic freedoms of this country; smash parliament, the free press, and the unions.

Well, what a load of rubbish. What a lie.

Our aim, unlike their aim, is not destruction. Our aim's making strong. We don't want weaker institutions, we want stronger.

We want a stronger press — a press that will reflect the real wishes of the vast majority, and not the liberal mewlings of a cosmopolitan élite. And we want stronger unions, strong enough to purge the wreckers in their midst, and battle for the real interests of their members. And we want stronger government — a government that has the power and will to do what needs to be done. And we want to see both capital and labour, all our institutions, serve not group, not section, most of all, not class, but the nation, and the race.

And so, I ask you — who's the real revolutionaries? Them — or us?

Applause, but also heckling. A chant from the HECKLERS: *'Nation Forward, Nazi Party.' It's drowned by the singing of 'Land of Hope and Glory'. Sounds of violence, chairs being turned over. The* HECKLERS *attempt the Internationale. It's drowned by a much louder chant, as sounds of violence grow: 'The Reds, the Reds, we gotta get rid of the Reds.' The spot on* TURNER *fades, as his face progresses from triumph to alarm. Blackout as the chants and sounds of violence go on growing till, suddenly, they cut out, and two single rifle shots are heard.*

Scene Eight

Lights. ROLFE *stands. He is in a dark overcoat, over a suit which shows signs of hasty travel. The stage is empty, though we are in fact in the Army HQ, Lisburn, Northern Ireland.* ROLFE *holds a union jack, crumpled, in his hands. He almost cradles it, as he would a baby. He looks up at the audience.*

ROLFE. There is a moment in one's life, more terrible, traumatic, even than the ending of a first love, or the consciousness of failed ambition, or awareness of the fact of growing old. It is the moment when you realise you have more time, regard, respect, for those who are your enemies than those you view as friends. That moment came to me at night, while sitting in an aeroplane, and flying northwards, west, across the Irish Sea, to fetch the body of my son.

He was, they told me, on the Lower Falls. Arms raid, just turned his head, a second. And the little boy, the schoolkid at the tenth floor window, with his sniper's gun, aimed just above the hairline, dead on true. Probably been there for hours. Waiting for that second. Patiently.

And on the plane, I realised, I had more time for him, the
12-year-old boy killer in the Divis Flats, the dark child with
his Russian rifle, far more time for him, than they. The
Generals. The Ministers. Assured us that the sun would never
set. The Generals, could not prevent my son, in his high
morning, his sun going down.

Yet you still won't see.

Will you? You generals, you ministers, police-chiefs, you won't
see, we are at war. Same war. In Belfast. Bradford. Bristol,
Birmingham, the one we lost in Bombay thirty years ago, the
one we're going to lose in Britain now. Unless you see in time.

Not thugs or lunatics, nor dupes of Moscow. They are
ordinary men and women, sane and normal, thousands of
them. And there is no time. They're everywhere. Deep, deep,
inside the gut. There is no time.

He is crying.

The sun has set. And we should not remember. We should
not look back, but should, instead, think only of the
morning.

He looks at the crumpled flag.

His fault. He turned his back.

The tears stop. ROLFE *raises the flag, holding it in a high
salute.*

We need an iron dawn.

He stands there, holding up the flag. Lights fade to darkness.

ACT THREE

'The misshapen hulk of the modern democratic state poses a serious
serious threat to the ideals that it was originally intended to serve.
The tentacles of bureaucracy and egalitarian socialism are
strangling private enterprise.'

> Robert Moss,
> in *The Collapse of Democracy*,
> 1975

'Private enterprise cannot be maintained in the age of Democracy;
it is conceivable only if the people have a sound idea of authority
... All the wordly goods which we possess, we owe to the
struggle of the chosen.'

> Adolf Hitler,
> 20 February 1933

Act Three

Scene One

House-lights down. A baby is crying. A doorbell rings, twice. Lights. CLIFTON's living room. A sofa, chair, coffee-table, on it dirty cups, glasses, a bottle of whisky, a telephone. Letters, documents, newspapers and children's toys on the floor. CLIFTON has switched the light on. He's in a dressing gown. He goes and answers the door. The baby's crying fades. Outside the door is CROSBY, muffled against the cold.

CROSBY. Hallo.

CLIFTON (*surprised*). Hallo.

CROSBY. I wondered if I could have a word.

CLIFTON. It's rather late.

CROSBY. It's rather urgent.

Slight pause.

CLIFTON. Do come in.

CLIFTON *admits* CROSBY, *closes the door.*

CROSBY. I'm sorry about the time.

CLIFTON. Well, we were up anyway. The baby.

Pause.

Drink? I'm afraid I've only got scotch.

CROSBY. Lovely.

CLIFTON. Lovely. (*He pours whiskies, gives one to* CROSBY. *Pause.*) What a nasty day it's been.

CROSBY. I'm sorry. It's a social situation on which Emily Poste is sadly mute. The proper etiquette on taking cocktails with one's class enemy at one in the morning.

CLIFTON (*smiles, sits*). What do you want?

CROSBY. I want to collaborate.

Enter SANDY, *wearing a nightie.*

SANDY. Hallo —

CROSBY. Hallo.

CLIFTON. Ruth OK?

SANDY. Fine. She was hungry. Look, if it's not impolitic to ask —

CLIFTON (*stands*). I'm sorry. Peter Crosby, Tory candidate. My wife.

SANDY. I do have a name, Bob. And being your wife isn't the sum total of my existence.

CLIFTON. I'm sorry. Sandy. Who works for the Thawston Community Project and is, in her spare time, my wife.

SANDY (*sits*). Thank you. Hallo.

CROSBY. I'm pleased to meet you.

Pause. SANDY *waves at* CROSBY, *to sit. He sits. Pause.*

SANDY. Well, what a privilege. To be the witness to a cross-bench hobnob. What I think is known, in parliamentary parlance, as the 'usual channels'. Right?

CROSBY (*smiles*). That's right.

CLIFTON (*sits*). OK, then. What d'you want?

CROSBY. Yuh.

Slight pause.

You know they're coming out, tomorrow, the Asians at Barons?

CLIFTON. Yup. I do.

CROSBY. And that the whites'll try and break the picket?

CLIFTON. Yup again.

Pause.

CROSBY. Look, Bob. I'll be quite open. As you know, both parties, have traditionally attempted, well, to keep race out of politics. Put up a kind of — common front against the sort of demagogy that Nation Forward's using over Barons. Now, I just felt, it might be, both our interests, to declare this strike, well, out of bounds politically. . . For just the last three days. To — try and, salvage . . . Well. You know.

Slight pause.

That's all.

CLIFTON. You want it out of bounds.

CROSBY. That's right.

CLIFTON. Mm.

CROSBY. Well?

CLIFTON. Well, the common front. On race. Your deal, in '62. Then ours, a higher bid, the Kenyan Asians Bill, restricting entry purely on the grounds of colour. So, not to be outdone, the stakes go higher, back to you in '71, Keep Race out of Politics, Keep Blacks out of Britain.

CROSBY. Well, yes, but —

CLIFTON. But some people who won't play that poker game — who stick their necks out. I like to think I'm one of them. In fact, had quite a postbag on the subject. (*He picks up a pile of letters, waves them.*) Not just from the public, either. Party workers, saying they won't canvass. So, when you talk about mutual benefits, I would but mention that I've already made my stand. Selling out now won't help me one iota. You, on the other hand —

CROSBY. Well, I'm sorry, I'd hoped you'd take a more moderate . . .

CLIFTON. Oh, for —

CROSBY (*stands*). All right.

Slight pause.

You heard about Nation Forward's meeting? What they said?

CLIFTON. I heard.

CROSBY. And what they did? To hecklers?

CLIFTON. Yuh, that too.

Pause.

CROSBY. Well, then. Goodnight.

CLIFTON. I'll see you Thursday.

CROSBY. Yes. (*He puts down his empty glass.*) Thanks for the scotch.

CLIFTON. Don't mention it.

Exit CROSBY.

SANDY. Poor little man.

CLIFTON. Why?

SANDY. Charity. He's going to lose his uncle's seat.

CLIFTON (*stands*). I wouldn't bet on it. At the moment, it's a race to see which of us loses most to Nation Forward.

Pause.

SANDY. But of course you're right.

CLIFTON. Sometimes I wonder.

SANDY. Like when?

CLIFTON (*pouring another drink*). Like when I'm on the doorstep, confronting the massed Alf Garnetts of the West Midlands. (*Accent.*) Oh, ar, Mr Clifton, we're with you on import controls, gotta be right, but it's the darkies, i'n'it? I mean to say, we know they live twenty to a room and breed like flies and don't use toilet tissue —

SANDY. Shut up, Bob.

CLIFTON. Why?

SANDY. Cos you're making me angry.

CLIFTON. Why?

SANDY. Because you've no right to patronise people you know nothing about.

Pause.

CLIFTON. Oh, come on, love, I've just had Peter Crosby —

SANDY. I just get a little fed up with your assumptions about people you meet for two minutes on a doorstep once in a blue moon. Because, unlike you, I actually work in the field, and I meet ordinary people all the time.

CLIFTON. Well, bully for you.

SANDY. Working-class people.

CLIFTON. Even bullier.

SANDY. And if you don't think there are real problems in integrating large numbers of people from a totally different cultural background then you need your head examining.

Slight pause.

CLIFTON. Oh, sure, dead right. And so . . . This week control, next week call a halt, week after send 'em back —

SANDY. You do annoy me sometimes, Bob —

CLIFTON. Love, we're both tired —

SANDY. I'm not tired.

Pause.

CLIFTON. Um, to what do I owe . .

SANDY (*angry now*). Look, Bob. You make your great bloody statements about unrestricted immigration and institutional racism. Well, you can afford to.

CLIFTON. I can't, that's exactly —

SANDY. You can afford to. But you just take a walk, leave the car for once, take a walk round West Thawston. You might even stop occasionally and actually listen to what people are saying. You know, listen? Then you might find out.

CLIFTON. I know —

SANDY. You don't know, so I'll tell you. Widow I visit. Only white face in the street. No English shops any more. Can't buy an English newspaper. The butcher's gone. The kids smash up her windows. Yes, of course, you'll say, all kids do that, but when the street was white it didn't happen, Bob. So I call her a 'racist'?

CLIFTON. No —

SANDY. Old man. 'Bout 60. A T&G shop steward who refused to take a cut in bonus rates. What happened? Got the push, his job went to a Pakistani. He's a fascist?

CLIFTON. You know the answer. They're blaming the wrong people.

SANDY. Who should they blame? Themselves?

CLIFTON (*as much for his own benefit as hers*). You know perfectly well. That there was bad housing long before they came. That the worst housing in Britain's in Glasgow, with hardly any blacks. That the years of highest immigration were the years of fullest employment. That the people who are responsible for unemployment and bad housing are bosses and property sharks and very few of them are black. You know that. So why —

SANDY. Oh, great. Pavlov reaction. It's the system. So what do I do? Lead them to the bloody barricades?

SANDY. Well —

Crash, offstage.

SANDY. What's that?

The phone rings.

CLIFTON. You answer it.

CLIFTON *goes.* SANDY *picks up the phone.*

SANDY. Hallo? Paul. What? No, he's . . . All right. I'll tell him.

She puts down the phone, goes to exit, meets CLIFTON *who enters holding a piece of paper. He stops her going through.*

CLIFTON. I've checked. Ruth's all right. It's a brick through the window. And stuff, through — on the carpet.

SANDY. Stuff?

CLIFTON. Excrement. Human, shit.

SANDY. Oh Christ.

CLIFTON (*gives her the note*). And this.

SANDY (*reads*). Take care of your snivelling little whore-spawned bastard Clifton the dark nights are coming.

CLIFTON. 'Whore' as in 'H.O.A.R'.

SANDY. But not a bad stab at 'snivelling'.

CLIFTON. Who was that on the phone?

SANDY. Paul. He's heard Nation Forward are going to be at Barons, first thing. Breaking the picket.

Pause.

CLIFTON. Now that is all we need. (*He sits.*) Another uncompromising stance? And hallo Peter Crosby, Honourable Member.

SANDY (*kneels beside* CLIFTON, *takes his hand. Very gently*). Bob. Once — you may remember, you said, about the Party. Why you're in it.

CLIFTON. Mm?

SANDY. You said, despite — oh, all the right wingers, all the selling out, you said at least, at least there was a chance of changing things. Of, really, changing things. You could have joined some, tiny, fringe, some two-horsed revolution, kept your ideas pure, you said, but at the price of never being any real use to anyone. You wished to be of use, you said, with all the compromise, retreat, the scorn that that implies.

CLIFTON *looks at* SANDY.

And that struck me as being rather brave.

CLIFTON *smiles at* SANDY.

Let's go to bed.

Slight pause.

CLIFTON. OK.

CLIFTON *stands and goes.* SANDY *moves to go, turns, looks round the room. She switches out the light.*

Scene Two

Dim lights. Outside the Foundry. Near the gates, KHERA, PATEL, PAUL, *perhaps other* PICKETS. *Placards:* DO NOT CROSS PICKET LINE, OUR FIGHT IS YOUR FIGHT, DON'T SCAB. *A few moments, then:*

KHERA (*out front*). Seven a.m. A winter's morning, picket line. For most of us, the first. And some surprise, we're doing it at all.

Enter PLATT *and a Police* INSPECTOR, *with possibly, other* POLICE *on one side of the stage.* KHERA *looks at them.*

But here we are.

He joins the other PICKETS.

PATEL (*to* PAUL). Police, with Platt.

PAUL. You bet.

PATEL *goes over to* KHERA, *talks to him.*

PLATT. They'll be here soon.

INSPECTOR. They will.

PLATT. Your tactics?

INSPECTOR. Keep well out. Long as they keep to peaceful giving or obtaining information, peaceful persuasion to work or not.

PLATT. Is that the law?

INSPECTOR. That is the law. I know their rights.

KHERA (*to* PAUL). What are they saying?

PAUL. I can't hear.

PLATT (*pointing at* PATEL). You see that one? The young one? He's the lad I mentioned.

INSPECTOR. Yes?

PLATT. With the interesting past.

Enter CLEAVER *and* LIZ, *the other side of the stage.*

KHERA. Nation Forward?

PATEL. Think it is.

PATEL *has a word with* PAUL, *who nods.*

INSPECTOR. And who are they?

PLATT. Dunno. Perhaps they're passers-by.

INSPECTOR. At seven in the morning? Passers-by?

PLATT. It's possible.

Enter TURNER *and* TONY, *with union jacks.*

INSPECTOR. With union jacks?

PLATT. I'm wrong. That's Turner. Nation Forward.

INSPECTOR. So it is.

PAUL (*to* PATEL). That's Turner.

PATEL. Yes.

KHERA. What now?

PATEL. Just wait.

Enter ATTWOOD *to centre stage.*

OK.

The PICKET *forms.*

PLATT. You're doing nothing?

INSPECTOR. As I said. We wait for an offence.

Pause. Then ATTWOOD *looks at his watch.*

ATTWOOD. Well. Half-past seven. Time for work. (*He walks to the* PICKETS.) Oh now look at this. (NATION FORWARD *move closer to* PICKETS.)

An unofficial picket-line.

The PICKETS *move closer together.*

Barring my path to work.

Pause.

Please let me pass. (*Suddenly, pulling at* KHERA.) Come on, Harry Krishna. Clear my road.

Freeze action.

KHERA. And I nearly did. When he said move, I nearly did, as reflex action, move to let him through. But then —

PATEL (*to* ATTWOOD). You scab.

KHERA. And then again —

PATEL (*pushing* ATTWOOD). You bastard scab.

KHERA. And then again.

PATEL (*pushing* ATTWOOD). You bastard blackleg scab.

ATTWOOD. Get your filthy hands off me, you dirty nig black scum.

PATEL (*takes* ATTWOOD *by the throat*). The name. The name's Prakash Patel. And, brother, we are staying in your road.

Freeze breaks.

PLATT (*quickly, marching over to the* PICKETS). Now, come on, lads, why not just let him through —

PATEL (*to* ATTWOOD, *referring to* PLATT). Now look, you, look. Look at his smiling face —

A whistle blows. NATION FORWARD *rush the* PICKETS *and blackout. At once, as pot hits* KERSHAW, *side of stage.*

KERSHAW. Unpleasant. But we got ten in. Unthinkable, to use these people, but. Impossible, not to. All other options closed. Unease, but then necessity. Better embrace the butcher, soil the bed, than perish with clean hands.

Blackout.

Scene Three

A police station. Most of the stage area is a corridor, lit. PAUL, *reading a crumpled newspaper, sits on a bench. To one side, an area representing an interview room. A* SUSPECT *sits at a table in this area, facing upstage. The* INSPECTOR *enters with* TONY.

INSPECTOR. There.

TONY *shrugs, sits on the bench. Exit* INSPECTOR. PAUL *puts down his paper, recognises* TONY.

PAUL. Tony.

TONY (*turns, recognises* PAUL). Paul.

Pause. It sinks in. They both laugh.

BOTH. Well, don't you meet —

TONY. People in the strangest places.

Pause. They laugh again.

PAUL. Well. How are you?

TONY. I'm fine. And you?

PAUL. Just, great, as well.

TONY. That's good.

PAUL. Apart, that is, from being stuck in here.

TONY. Ar. Right.

Pause.

PAUL (*mock confidential*). Um, look, bab, don't want to pry or anything, but, uh . . . what you doing here then?

TONY. Got arrested.

PAUL. Snap.

TONY. I'm waiting, to be charged.

PAUL. Well, snap again.

Slight pause.

Um — ?

TONY. Bit of aggro, up at Baron Castings.

Slight pause.

PAUL. Yuh?

TONY. You know, there's this dispute —

PAUL. Yes, sure, so . . . You were on picket line?

TONY. Of course I wasn't on the bloody picket line.

Slight pause.

Were there to break the bloody picket, weren't we?

PAUL. We?

TONY. Yuh, we. Nation Forward.

Pause.

PAUL. I was on the picket-line.

Pause. TONY laughs.

TONY. Oh, blimey —

PAUL. So what's funny?

TONY. Blimey. Paul McShane. Great fighter for the working-class. Siding with a gang of nigs to undercut the wages of his brother —

PAUL. Tony, that's a load —

TONY (*angry*). Why don't people ever realise? We didn't ask for it.

PAUL. For what?

TONY. Have Pakkies take our jobs and houses. Turning England's green and pleasant land into an Asian slum. We didn't —

PAUL. Green and pleasant? Yuh. Just like round here. With all them lovely trees and verdant foliage. You know, they had a poster in the war: This Is Your England, Fight For It. A picture of a village green. Thatched cottages. How many English soldiers died had ever seen a country cottage? Thatched or otherwise?

TONY. They did it, if you want to know, Paul, cos some people bat for their own side.

PAUL *laughs*.

PAUL. For Christ's sake, Tony, who have you been talking to?

TONY. No need to talk. I know it. Any white man knows it. In the blood.

PAUL. The blood?

TONY. The spirit of the Race.

Pause.

PAUL. Oh God. (*He stands and shouts off.*) Hey, Sergeant! Did you know, you got the bleeding Master Race in here? You can't do him for causing an affray . . .

Pause. PAUL *turns back to* TONY, *for his reaction.*

TONY (*quiet, calm*). You really don't know, do you?

PAUL. What?

TONY. Your real enemy.

PAUL. Well, actually, I do take the old-fashioned view, that for the working-class the enemy's —

TONY. Oh, ar. The bosses. Which?

PAUL. Well? Answer?

TONY. Have a sniff, Paul. Got a nose. Can smell the alien stink. Or can't you?

PAUL. Oh, sure, yuh, can do. Smell the foul stench of all those black speculators. Those Pakky stockbrokers. Jamaican Managing Directors.

TONY. Not them, Paul.

PAUL. No, not them. The Ruling Class.

TONY. No, Paul. The Ruling Race.

Pause.

PAUL. All history's the struggle of the classes.

TONY. No. All history's the struggle of the races.

Pause.

PAUL. The workers of all races must unite.

TONY. The workers of all classes must unite.

Pause.

PAUL. Come down to it, the choice is socialism or barbarity.

TONY. Come down to it, it's Zionism, One-World Tyranny, or us.

Slight pause. TONY *stands.*

And when we win, get rid of them, there'll be no need for conflict. Class war. Strikes, and all. Then capital and labour work together, in the interests of the nation. Putting Britain first. The nation, over all.

Pause.

'Course, you can sneer. At race and blood. But everything you got, Paul, comes from that. Everything healthy, worthy, everything with any meaning, value, s'from the blood. Cos seed don't die, what we are doesn't die. Passed on. From generations, passed on, from the legions of the dead to legions of the living, legions of the future.

PAUL. Tony, last time they said that, it ended up with putting people into —

TONY (*simply*). No, no, Paul. It never happened. Auschwitz, n'all. Just factories. The holocaust, just photos forged. Invented by the Jews.

PAUL *looks at* TONY. TONY *still.*

PAUL. You Nazi.

TONY. Yuh. That's right.

Suddenly, PAUL *out front.*

PAUL. And, you know, it was like looking in a mirror, looking at him, me old mate, Tony. All correct, the same, identical. Just one thing wrong. Left's right. Class — race. As different as can be. The opposite. The bleeding wrong way round . . .

Lights cross-cut to INSPECTOR *and* SUSPECT. *We now see the* SUSPECT *is* PATEL. INSPECTOR *holding an Indian passport.*

INSPECTOR. Right, Mr Patel. Let's go through it just once more. You claim you entered when?

Blackout.

Scene Four

Lights on a Pakistani restaurant. A couple of tables. CLIFTON *and* SANDY *are sitting eating.* PAUL *and* KHERA *have just come in, are standing.*

PAUL. They've arrested Prakash Patel.

CLIFTON. What?

PAUL. And they're reckoning to do me for assault.

Slight pause.

CLIFTON. Sit down.

PAUL *and* KHERA *sit.*

PAUL. Now look, Bob, if you rang the dailies, now, you could get a statement in tomorrow morning, demanding his release —

CLIFTON. Patel's being done for assault?

PAUL (*impatient*). No, he's —

CLIFTON. Thought you said —

KHERA. Illegal immigrant. Under the '71 Immigration Act. Easier than jailing strikers. Just fly them back to India.

SANDY. But there's an amnesty.

KHERA. It doesn't cover. He's an overstayer, came in as a student, just didn't go back.

CLIFTON. Poor sod.

PAUL. So you see, Bob, it'd be great, day before polling —

CLIFTON. Where is he?

PAUL. At the copshop.

CLIFTON. And they found out —

PAUL. Platt. It has to be. The bastard knew, and shopped him.

CLIFTON (*non-commital*). Yuh.

Slight pause.

PAUL. Well?

CLIFTON (*businesslike*). Right. Now, he's an overstayer, yuh?

PAUL. Well, so they say.

CLIFTON. But he is?

PAUL. Well, I suppose so.

CLIFTON. So, in fact, he's breaking the law.

Pause.

PAUL. Well, yuh —

CLIFTON. Now that does make it rather difficult.

PAUL. Why?

SANDY. Because, if he's breaking the law, Bob obviously can't demand his release.

PAUL. Why not?

SANDY. Obviously.

Pause.

PAUL (*to* CLIFTON). But it's just what you been saying all along. Oppose the Immigration Act.

SANDY. That's not what you're asking him to do.

PAUL. Yes, it is. Here's a case, a guy —

SANDY. Bob's asking for the law to be changed, not broken.

Pause.

PAUL (*to* CLIFTON). Well, say something.

CLIFTON. What do you want me to say.

PAUL. Well, actually, that your good lady is talking through the back of her neck.

Pause.

CLIFTON. She isn't.

PAUL. Oh, I see.

CLIFTON. No you don't. So I'll explain.

PAUL. I'm all ears.

Slight pause. Strain in CLIFTON's *voice.*

CLIFTON. Now. I'm standing for election as a legislator, right? That is the job-description. And I'm doing that, can only do that, if I believe that laws should be made, OK? And that it's possible to change society by making them.

PAUL. But —

CLIFTON. So how, if that has any meaning, can I say that once they're made we shouldn't keep them?

PAUL. Well, what 'bout me? Assault, on Fascists.

SANDY. Paul, the law can't not protect a guy just cos you happen to regard him as a Fascist.

Pause.

CLIFTON. It's just a matter, simple, of the rule of law.

SANDY. You've got to see the problem, Paul.

PAUL. I can. I'm talking to it. It's sitting there, stuffing its face with chicken byriani.

Pause.

CLIFTON. The law's a car, Paul. Goes whichever way you steer it.

PAUL. So why, whoever's driving, does it always go one way?

Pause.

KHERA. There is a story, 'bout the rule of law. In Amritsar. 1919. A Brigadier-General, Dyer, ordered his troops to fire on a crowd of unarmed Indian demonstrators. Nearly 400 killed. Facts took some time to come out. Then, of course, Dyer was investigated. Strict legality. Censured. Asked to resign.

SANDY (*quietly*). 1919.

KHERA. That massacre. Defence of British rule in India.

SANDY (*quietly*). Which ended thirty years ago.

KHERA. Oh, yes, of course. I'm sorry.

Slight pause. As he speaks, softly, KHERA *looks at no-one, perhaps just playing with the ashtray on the table.*

I come from Jullundur, the Punjab. Sikh upbringing. Train the children to be quiet, subservient, respectful. So, to England, land of tolerance and decency, and found it hard to understand. But last year, I went home, on holiday, to India. Saw, with new eyes, just what the English did. And then I understood. There is more British capital in India, today, than 30 years ago.

It runs quite deep. Even the poor, white British, think that they, not just their masters, born to rule. And us, the blacks, the Irish, all of us — a lesser breed, without the Rule of Law.

But that's your problem.

He stands. To SANDY.

You'll forgive me. I'm on picket duty, seven in the morning. (*He goes.*)

Long pause.

PAUL. Well, that's put you —

CLIFTON. Did you see Crosby, in the Evening Post? Feared some of his remarks might have been misinterpreted. Wanted to make it clear, completely opposed to any further coloured immigration. Already signs of, social strain.

PAUL. Well, by tomorrow, there'll be one less, won't there?

Slight pause.

Ar, I saw it.

CLIFTON (*hands* PAUL *a note*). You won't have seen this. Came through the window last night. Accompanied by a brick and a neat little pile of excreta.

PAUL *reads the note.*

PAUL. So you retreat? Because of this? You see what these bastards can do, and you retreat?

SANDY. Ruth's eight months old, Paul.

PAUL. Oh, ar. And doubtless the law will give her every protection.

CLIFTON (*loses his temper*). You know, sometimes, Paul, your self-righteousness reaches a pitch of messianic fervour that I find quite terrifying.

PAUL. Oh, ar?

CLIFTON. Ar. And that's surprising. Because what you're doing isn't very difficult. It's rather easy, comfortable, your anger, rather cosy, in its steel-eyed way. Because you think in absolutes, in dogmas, you needn't face the real fights, the real, mucky struggles, you keep clean. And if your — sterile constructs ever touch the real world and its diseases, they're cocooned in rubber, scrubbed a thousand times, to keep them pure.

Pause.

PAUL (*quietly, gently, a genuine need to explain*). You know, there's a funny moment, comes to you, you see your real friends. Came to me, a meeting of the Barons strikers. Oh, yuh, sure, all clenched fists and synthetic Maoist fervour.

Just, amid all that, some people learning. Talking, for the first time, 'bout just how to do it, working out, quite slowly, tortuously, quite frustrating, you know, for us old pros, to sit there and listen to it all.

But it is listening to people grow. Learning that it's possible for them to make their future. Bit like the morning. Sun comes up, so slow, can't see it's changing. But it's growing lighter. Think of that.

Their fault. No turning back. The need, to be our own. To change, the real world.

He stands.

Tara.

Exit PAUL.

SANDY. Well done.

CLIFTON. Hm. In two days' time we'll know. What profits it a man to lose his party's soul.

SANDY. You haven't.

CLIFTON. Well, I didn't have much choice.

SANDY. You did.

CLIFTON. Well, still.

Slight pause.

I better win.

Blackout.

Scene Five

In the darkness, we hear the voice of the MAYORESS *of Taddley, through a mike.*

MAYORESS'S VOICE. I, the undersigned, being the Returning Officer for the Parliamentary Constituency of Taddley, hereby give notice that the total number of votes cast for each candidate was as follows:

Lights. The Election Result. Standing from left to right: CLEAVER, TONY, TURNER, PLATT, EMMA, CROSBY, MAYORESS, WILCOX, CLIFTON, SANDY, PAUL *and* KHERA. *The first three and last two slightly apart.* EMMA *is* CROSBY's *wife,* WILCOX *is a Liberal. As the* MAYORESS *announces the result,* PLATT *and* SANDY *note the figures down. A* VOICE *identifies the candidates.*

MAYORESS. Clifton, Robert John —

VOICE. Labour.

MAYORESS. Ten thousand and ninety-six.

A splatter of applause. CLIFTON *looks worried, the* TORIES *pleased.*

Crosby, Peter Sanderson —

VOICE. Conservative.

MAYORESS. Eleven thousand —

Big applause. CROSBY *can't believe it.* EMMA *kisses him.* CLIFTON *shakes his hand.* MAYORESS *attempts.*

Eleven thousand, eight hundred and thirty-two; Turner, Dennis . . . Turner, Dennis . . .

Applause dies.

Turner, Dennis Stephen —

VOICE. Nation Forward.

Sudden burst of chanting: 'Nation Forward, Nazi Party'. Dies.

MAYORESS. Six thousand nine hundred and ninety-three.

Applause. Booing. NATION FORWARD *look delighted.*

Wilcox, Diana —

VOICE. Liberal.

MAYORESS. One thousand and fifty-two.

A little applause. SANDY *gives* CLIFTON *the note and kisses him.* CROSBY, PLATT *and* EMMA *confer. As:*

And that the undermentioned person has been duly elected to serve as member for the said constituency: Peter Sanderson Crosby.

She turns to CROSBY, *shakes his hand.* CROSBY *taking over the mike, as* CLIFTON *speaks to* PLATT.

CLIFTON. Well done, Jim. Think we can conclude, they won you the election.

PLATT. Only if, took more from you than us, Bob. And who knows where the buggers come from.

CROSBY (*down the microphone*). Um —

Snap blackout. A very short time. Lights. The central section of people, and the microphone, have gone. Those left — TONY, CLEAVER *and* TURNER *on one side,* PAUL *and* KHERA *on the other, are left looking at the place where* CROSBY *stood. Then, as the lights fade down to dim, night lighting, the two groups become aware of each other. Edgy. Nervy. Then, on* PAUL *and* KHERA's *side, blocking their exit,* ATTWOOD *enters.* KHERA *and* PAUL *move towards centre. Pause. Then,* CLEAVER *taps* TURNER *on the shoulder, makes to go.* TURNER *not going.* CLEAVER *gestures him to follow.* TURNER *follows* CLEAVER *out.*

TONY. Well, here we are.

PAUL (*to* KHERA, *makes to go*). Come on.

TONY. Hi, Paul.

PAUL (*to* KHERA). Come on, mate.

TONY. And hallo, Paul's pet monkey.

Slight pause.

KHERA (*to* PAUL). No.

TONY. OK.

> TONY *goes for* KHERA, PAUL *to protect him,* ATTWOOD *for* PAUL. *Before he can get to* TONY, PAUL *aware of* ATTWOOD, *turns and knees him as* TONY *knocks* KHERA *down.* ATTWOOD *doubles up,* TONY *about to kick* KHERA *when he hears two clicks.* TONY *turns, thinking they come from behind him.*

TONY. Wha —

> *Quickly,* KHERA *slides one of the two flick-knives he holds across the floor to* PAUL. TONY *and* ATTWOOD *realise.* PAUL *picks up the knife, slashes at* ATTWOOD, *who manages to avoid the knife and runs out.* TONY *tries to stamp on* KHERA's *hand, misses.* KHERA *up, slashes at* TONY's *face,* TONY *turns to run, faces* PAUL. *He stops. Blood is beginning to run down his cheek.* TONY *is looking very, very scared.*

KHERA. Right. Now tell me. Who you think you're doing all this for.

> *Blackout.*

Scene Six

Lights on a hospitality room in a merchant bank in the City of London. Leather chairs. On the wall, a huge, dark painting of the putting down of the Indian Mutiny. CLEAVER *sits.* TURNER *stands, looking at the picture. A moment or two. Then* CLEAVER *looks at his watch.* TURNER *touches the picture, feeling its texture. Then he turns to* CLEAVER.

CLEAVER. He said they might be late. A meeting — implications of the Deutschmark doing something or other.

TURNER. Oh, ar?

CLEAVER. Yes.

> TURNER *back to the painting.* CLEAVER *stands, goes to* TURNER.

TURNER. I was there, you know.

CLEAVER (*smiling*). In 1857?

TURNER. No, from 1945. In Calcutta, bastards stoned us. Lot of lads, the troops, you know, refused to fire. They saw it

as a kind of, justified revenge. (*He nods to the painting.*)
You know, for that, and all.

CLEAVER. Guilt complex. Liberal masochism. What we've got
to —

TURNER. Oh, sure. It makes you sick.

Slight pause.

D'you suppose they'll —

Enter KERSHAW, ROLFE and CAROL, ROLFE's secretary.

KERSHAW. Richard, I'm sorry.

CLEAVER. Doesn't matter.

KERSHAW. Richard, this is Lewis Rolfe.

ROLFE *and* CLEAVER *shake hands.*

CLEAVER.) How d'you do.
ROLFE.   ) Hallo.

KERSHAW. And Dennis Turner, Lewis, who I think you've met.

ROLFE (*to* TURNER, *shaes his hand*). Indeed. Long time ago.
Congratulations, Dennis.

TURNER. Thank you, sir.

ROLFE (*smiles*). No need for that.

KERSHAW. Well. 23 per cent. You'll be delighted.

TURNER. Well, low poll. But it's a start.

CLEAVER. A deposit saved is a deposit earned.

All smile.

ROLFE. Carol, any chance of sherry??

CAROL. Yes, of course. (*She goes.*)

ROLFE. Do, please sit.

All sit, except ROLFE.

KERSHAW (*to* TURNER). I imagine Richard's filled you in?

TURNER. He has.

Slight pause.

KERSHAW. Well, then.

CLEAVER. We need to know your reasons.

KERSHAW. Yes, of course.

Enter CAROL *with a tray of sherry which she passes round. Then she goes out.*

ROLFE. Right, gentlemen. In answer to your question.

Slight pause.

We are under threat. The British Nation, and its enterprise. The two are indivisible. A blow at one's a blow against the other. We face a common threat, we face a common enemy. We have a common need.

A glue. To stick the nation to itself. And, yes, to make its enterprise secure. Unite the Durham miner with the Surrey stockbroker. The East End navvy with the Scottish laird. An ideology.

We know what we've been offered. Liberalism. From whatever source. A community of tolerance, compassion, moderation. Tolerance of crime, permissiveness. Compassion for the multi-coloured misfits of the world. And moderation, military reserve, low profile, in the face of insurrection. To a point when gangrene's gone so deep that — we must think about extremes.

You offer an extreme. An old idea. Not merely nation. Race. Roots deeply twined into the universal gut. To bind the barrel fast with hoops of steel.

Not pale. Not weak. Not atrophied. Red, white and blue — in tooth and claw. (*Half-smiling.*) Mm?

CLEAVER. There's more to it than that, of course.

KERSHAW. Fighting the Reds, wherever they appear. The schools, the factories.

CLEAVER. Why not the police?

KERSHAW. The police don't know. They're isolated. You — the Reds are on your streets. You know.

CLEAVER. The army?

ROLFE. Can contain, perhaps. They can't destroy.

CLEAVER. We also combat international capital.

KERSHAW. We also need protection.

CLEAVER. If it means control?

ROLFE. You scratch us, we'll scratch you.

CLEAVER. You'd sacrifice the 'free' of enterprise?

KERSHAW. Yes, to preserve the privacy of property.

> *Pause.*

One doesn't, like, the dentist.

> *Slight pause.*

But to save the tooth.

ROLFE. Physicians. Army, police. Just tranquilize, to numb the pain. You — surgeons. Use the passions. And rechannel the hot blood, and send it gushing down another artery.

> *Pause.*

CLEAVER. Conditions.

KERSHAW. One. The tendency, among your people, shall we say, a little far to port?

CLEAVER. Oh, yes. David Maxwell's little gang of Racial Trotskyites.

> *Slight pause.*

Not any more.

KERSHAW. I see.

> *Pause.*

CLEAVER. And then?

ROLFE. We felt, by bankers' order. Quietly. No more, yet, than insurance. Down payment, on a possible tomorrow.

CLEAVER. When you say 'we'?

ROLFE. Both personally, and on behalf.

KERSHAW. United Vehicles.

ROLFE. The Metropolitan Investment Trust.

CLEAVER. How much?

> TURNER *looks up at* ROLFE.

TURNER. What did you say?

ROLFE. I'm sorry?

TURNER. What's your firm?

ROLFE. The Metropolitan Investment Trust.

KERSHAW. Shall we continue over lunch?

CLEAVER (*stands*). Why not.

ROLFE. Let's go.

He gestures the COMPANY *out.* CLEAVER, KERSHAW *and* ROLFE *exit, leaving* TURNER, *who is forgotten in the general exodus. As they go,* ROLFE *to* CLEAVER, *conversationally.*

ROLFE. I thought we'd try a new place on Cornhill. That's if you don't mind Italian . . .

They're gone. TURNER *goes and looks at the painting. Enter* CAROL, *with a tray, to collect the sherry glasses.*

CAROL. Oh, I'm sorry. I thought you'd all —

TURNER. They have.

CAROL. Are you not lunching?

TURNER. No.

Slight pause.

CAROL. Fine.

TURNER *is still looking at the painting.* CAROL *collects the sherry glasses. When she's finished, to* TURNER, *conversationally, about the painting.*

CAROL. Ghastly, isn't it?

TURNER. It's him.

CAROL. I'm sorry?

TURNER. Didn't realise. Your boss.

CAROL. My boss?

TURNER. That he's the Metropolitan Investment Trust.

CAROL. I don't quite see —

TURNER. The people took my livelihood away.

Slight pause.

You may not notice it. I'm suffering a gross deficiency of greed.

Slight pause.

You're right.

CAROL. What's right?

TURNER. It's ghastly.

Enter CLEAVER.

CLEAVER. Dennis? What's the matter? Aren't you coming?

TURNER. No.

CAROL. He said — we took his livelihood —

CLEAVER *gestures* CAROL *to go. She exits.* CLEAVER *to* TURNER.

CLEAVER. Dennis. It doesn't matter. All that's in the past.

The future, Dennis, that's what matters. Money. Power. Opportunity. The cause. Not might, not could, not will. It is happening here.

And what can stop us now?

A long, long pause. TURNER *doesn't know what to say. He stares at the painting. Then, finally, he turns back to* CLEAVER.

TURNER. Tell me.

Suddenly, light change. CLEAVER *and* TURNER *lit from behind, in silhouette. A* VOICE *is heard; gentle, quiet, insistent. It is the voice of* ADOLF HITLER.

ADOLF HITLER. Only one thing could have stopped our Movement: if our adversaries had understood its principle, and had smashed, with the utmost brutality, the nucleus of our new Movement.

Slight pause.

Hitler. Nuremburg. Third of September, 1933.

Blackout.